DRIVEN

DRIVEN

HOW TO SUCCEED IN BUSINESS AND IN LIFE

ROBERT HERJAVEC

with John Lawrence Reynolds

HarperCollins Publishers Ltd

HarperCollins books may be purchased for educational, business,
or sales promotional use through our Special Markets Department.

HarperCollins Publishers Ltd
2 Bloor Street East, 20th Floor
Toronto, Ontario, Canada
M4W 1A8

www.harpercollins.ca

Library and Archives Canada Cataloguing in Publication

Herjavec, Robert
Driven : how to succeed in business
and in life / Robert Herjavec.

ISBN 978-1-55468-708-4

1. Self-actualization (Psychology). 2. Success in
business. 3. Success. I. Title.

BF637.S8H399 2010   158.1   C2010-900515-5

Printed and bound in the United States

RRD 9 8 7 6 5 4 3 2 1

For my late parents (Katica and Vladimir),
without whose sacrifice I would not be here.

For my family—Diane, Brendan, Skye and Caprice—whose
support and love makes the journey worthwhile and joyous.

CONTENTS

DRIVEN

1

Know a Good Deal When You See It

The $200,000 cheque was on the table and we were ready to sign the deal.

Four bright young guys had achieved what thousands of entrepreneurs only dream of: they had obtained venture capital to transform their company from a struggling concept to a potentially major corporation, thanks to the cash that was almost in their hands and the expertise of their new partners, who happened to be all five panellists on the CBC-TV show *Dragons' Den*. Including me.

The young men named their company JobLoft and their vision was sound: develop an Internet-based service to connect hospitality and retail-oriented companies in need of qualified people, charging a fee for the service. Instead of using newspaper advertisements or employment agencies, both of which are time-consuming and expensive, employers and prospective employees would connect through JobLoft. The founders wisely narrowed their focus to target firms with a 67-per-cent annual staff turnover, precisely the kind of companies interested in satisfying their staffing requirements quickly and often.

We liked the concept, we liked what they had achieved, we liked the prospects for growth, and we liked the four young men, all of them wearing orange ties, who brought the critical intangibles of dedication and enthusiasm to the mix. Jim Treliving, who launched and still runs Boston Pizza, and Laurence Lewin, whose La Senza chain of stores was becoming a dominant force in lingerie sales, were especially enthusiastic. Their participation alone would add a wealth of expertise in guiding the growth of JobLoft.

All five of us on *Dragons' Den* agreed to contribute $40,000 each to the investment, buying 50 per cent of the company with the $200,000 total. Such unanimity among us is unusual, and a measure of the venture's appeal. These guys making the pitch were good, and the Dragons were enthusiastic. Sounded like a win-win deal all around. So what happened?

Before the Dragons were to meet, sign the contracts and present them with the cheque, the young men decided to invite their silent partner—who happened to be their former business-school professor—to the ceremony. I suppose they wanted to share the glory of the moment with the person who, they believed, provided them with the inspiration for their business.

When the JobLoft partners arrived for the videotaped event, we didn't know what to make of the middle-aged man accompanying them. He wasn't dressed in the style you might expect for a serious business meeting. His worn leather jacket, open sport shirt and sandals hardly fit the mood, but we weren't going to stand on ceremony, and when he was introduced as their professor we acknowledged his presence and got started.

For the first few minutes, the professor stood aside, watching and listening with an expression that suggested he was suffering from indigestion. Finally, as I finished reviewing the deal with the young men who had pitched JobLoft to us, the professor barked an objection. "I don't like the business plan," he said, and launched into a critique of the strategy we had just agreed upon.

Well, all right. A business plan deserves to be examined from every angle before implementing it, and we listened to the professor's objections, most of them dealing with our proposed strategy to target employers over prospective hires. When we expressed disagreement with his concerns, the professor began questioning our academic credentials.

"Do you have a business degree?" he demanded.

What was his point? Is earning a business degree an assurance of success for entrepreneurs? Not really. I had successfully launched and managed companies dealing with Internet security and other computer-related aspects, but I achieved it without formal business training. Jim Treliving's early business training included experience as an RCMP officer, a career he abandoned in favour of delivering pizza orders from his car, which also served from time to time as his office and bedroom. From that start, he built a billion-dollar corporation. How many business-school graduates can make the same claim?

As though emboldened by our lack of academic credentials, the professor grew more strident in his objections, and began insisting that the Internet search engine that would connect the job openings and the job seekers be designed to his specifications.

Jim, who had mentioned earlier in the meeting that he had flown to the meeting on his private jet, interrupted the professor's harangue to say, "You know, I have no idea what you're talking about."

The professor fixed Jim with a scowl. "If you spent more time dealing with business instead of flying around on your jet," he sneered, "maybe you would know the answer."

I couldn't believe the man's arrogance. "Excuse me?" I asked, assuming he would express his point in a more polite manner.

He swung to face me. "You heard me," he snapped. "You guys should feel lucky you're making this investment in the company." Then he added: "Let's be honest. It's only $200,000, and that's not a lot of money to any of us."

"You know," I replied as I reached for the cheque, "maybe the problem is that I can still remember when $200,000 was all the money in the world." I held the cheque in the air for everyone to see. Then I tore it up and dropped the pieces on the table. "If it's such a small amount of money," I suggested to the professor, "why don't you put it in?"

As you can imagine, this distressed the young men who, a few moments earlier, had anticipated using the cash to expand their business. Now the cheque lay scattered like confetti on the floor, and access to industry contacts and experienced support that would have been available to them through Jim, me and the other Dragons had vanished.

I took no pleasure in tearing up the cheque. Like every other investment I made, I had planned to earn a profit from my share.

But I felt two lessons had to be learned in this situation. Lesson One: you don't bite the hand that feeds you. Venture capital is simply too difficult to obtain, especially when it's accompanied by a sincere interest in helping entrepreneurs succeed. Lesson Two: Do not assume that every business idea you have is worth a million dollars on its own. Because it is not. Life is more complex than that. In addition, do not believe that academic training, as valuable as it might be in the right context, is more valuable than practical experience, especially when it involves launching, building and managing a business.

I felt for the young men who watched the investment money vanish after they had worked hard to acquire it. They had demonstrated the qualities that all successful entrepreneurs possess, including vision, determination and sufficient energy to make their concept a reality. What they also had, and didn't need, was a so-called silent partner who couldn't remain silent and keep his outlandish criticism and arrogant attitude to himself. Academics such as their professor may be good at delivering theory, but theory itself has no value, and using it as a weapon to shoot down practical experience is unacceptable. If the professor was going to influence the value and potential return of our investment, either he or our investment had to go. He appeared to be a permanent fixture. Our cash wasn't. So it was gone.

Experience Comes with a Price

Unlike the professor, whose views appeared to be rooted exclusively in academic concepts, mine were shaped by practical experience. As a university graduate, I have great respect for scholars and academics. And as a guy who built substantial family assets out of my determination to succeed, I recognize the limits of academic theory. Without the ability to visualize a goal and believe it will be reached, nothing of substance will be achieved. Not by anybody. Not at any time. Not in any place.

Here's the good news: the young men who made the mistake of bringing their know-it-all business professor along for the presentation were young enough to learn from their mistakes. And, as I'll demonstrate a few times on the following pages, we often learn more from our mistakes than from our successes.

By the way, their company, JobLoft, managed to grow and enjoy some success after I tore up the cheque, and it was later sold to a larger competitor, generating, I expect, a satisfying capital gain for the founders. The company may have grown faster and bigger with our injection of cash and reservoir of experience, but the event didn't destroy their dreams. Not by any means. Good for them.

If I had written this book before the incident involving the torn cheque and the challenging professor, the young men who launched JobLoft might have chosen not to bring their professor along to the meeting. They would, I hope, have recognized

that they possessed everything they needed to become successful entrepreneurs: a clear vision, a viable opportunity, an effective business model, a determination to succeed and, for a few
moments at least, a substantial amount of cash from a group of
interested, experienced and supportive investors.

They had, but didn't need, an academic who instead of influ-
encing aspects of their business insulted the source of their badly
needed investment capital. Looking back at that event, I wish I
had made two important points to the young men, points I cover
in this book.

The first would be to emphasize that $200,000 in investment
cash for companies whose founders had yet to prove themselves
in the down-and-dirty pit of business represented a rare opportunity. That kind of capital, provided by people who both mater-
ially and emotionally wanted to see the venture succeed, does not
fall into everyone's lap each day. I believe they understood this
point. As a result of my actions, they also learned that money—
and the support and interest of investors—can be as fleeting as
a leaf in the wind if things don't go well. Money travels to two
places: to where it is wanted and appreciated, and to where it is
likely to return with an acceptable profit.

My second point would go beyond the need for cash to the
true motivation for becoming an entrepreneur in the first place:
the overwhelming, often obsessive desire to bring a vision to life.
This desire is so powerful that it cannot be diverted or diluted
even by an awareness that the odds of success are against it, and
it is not enhanced with dreams of enormous wealth that the
venture may generate.

Successful businesspeople retain a quality most others not only lack but often fail to comprehend, and that's the unrelenting drive to convert a vision into reality. They are driven to realize this goal in a manner that appears to defy logic among others who lack this drive. The rewards make it all worthwhile. No true entrepreneur seriously regrets the sacrifice made to realize his or her dream. The decision has always been worth it, whether measured in dollars or in degrees of satisfaction.

I have gathered my personal experiences and observations in this book. I hope you find them enlightening and entertaining, whether you are driven to achieve the same level of success achieved by me and other inhabitants of the Dragons' Den, or are simply attempting to understand the motivation that powered them.

2

Appreciate What It Takes to Succeed

Whatever mistakes the young men behind JobLoft might have made, I admired them for having a dream and taking the initiative to make it a reality. On that basis alone, they were in the minority.

Most people look for security when it comes to choosing a career. They like the idea of knowing what they will be doing from 9 a.m. to 5 p.m. each working day and how much they will pocket from their paycheque each month. They value two or three or more weeks of paid vacation every year and the hopeful prospect of having steady employment all the way to their retirement years, whenever those arrive.

That's understandable, and I respect and value those who make that choice. But it was not my choice, nor is it the choice of people who appear on *Dragons' Den* in search of funding. No matter how badly conceived and poorly presented their ventures may be, I admire them for their determination to take risks and their preference to play the role of entrepreneur over that of employee.

The word *determination* may not quite do the job. During the economic downturn of 2008–09, anyone who chose to launch a new business had to be more than determined; they had to be almost insane. Yet people insisted on starting new companies, exploring new ventures and generally tossing aside the appeal of job security in favour of entrepreneurial success.

They weren't insane, of course; they were passionate about achieving their dream, and that's the line that separates them from everyone else. The very best of them will not only succeed in establishing a business and generating a profit from it, they will learn to adapt as the business evolves into something more established and vibrant, responding to changes in the economic environment. That's a difficult transition to master.

While the entrepreneurial spirit is most evident (and essential) among those who choose to launch their own business, it also represents a valuable trait in those who prefer to work within an existing corporation. Every successful corporate executive I have encountered shared the same entrepreneurial essence, the same drive to grow a business to the limits of their—and its—capacity, as me. How can you not admire that? How can you not believe that it is the essential core of success in a free-enterprise society? Striving to succeed in business according to your own talents and vision is a trait we should all value and promote in our friends, our families and especially ourselves.

My admiration for people who share this point of view was behind my decision to participate in *Dragons' Den*. I'm not there primarily to generate profits from the investments that I and other Dragons may agree to make. We're there to encounter real businesses with real cash flow and real ideas that can't get funding somewhere else. It's a great format for entrepreneurs to learn and possibly get funding. It's also a way of supporting the value of small businesses to the North American economy. Most people are aware that small businesses create the majority of new jobs. Events over the past few years, especially those concerning the antics of Wall Street and some of the more outrageous examples of unchecked greed and false values demonstrated by giant corporations, have underlined the importance of small businesses and the people who risk everything to help them succeed.

The Essential Companion to Passion: Communication

One of the least acknowledged essentials to success in business is the ability to communicate your concepts effectively to a wide range of people, including investors, employees and customers. No one is likely to surpass or even match the passion you feel for your venture, but the more of your vision you can transfer to these groups, the more likely your business will succeed.

Communicating your vision effectively differs from salesmanship or financial analysis, especially when dealing with potential investors. If you can't get me excited about your concept and its prospects, you face more than just the challenge of convincing me to hand over my money as an investment; you'll likely face the same challenge of convincing customers to hand over their money for your product or service.

That's always in the back of my mind, because I won't be running your company for you. You'll be doing that, and using my money to generate profit.

Think of all the different qualities involved: the ability to identify a business opportunity, the vision to shape it into a profitable venture, the passion to accept the risk involved in pursuing it, and the talent to communicate both the vision and your passion to others. That's a rare combination. With them, there is still no guarantee of success. Without them, however, there is no possibility.

3

Be Who You Are, Not Who You Think You Are

None of us on the panel of *Dragons' Den* set out to become performers on network television. We're all businesspeople at heart, geared to make decisions in relative privacy among partners, colleagues and customers. What are we doing discussing business in front of millions of strangers?

As much as we may try to deny it, we're performers of one kind or another. And we have difficulty turning down a challenge. The show also teaches us things that we can apply to business and to life. We learn about other business ventures, about the impact of culture and technology on the economy, and from time to time we learn something about ourselves as well.

"Nobody Tells Me to Be Quiet!"

I arrived at my office one day in 2006 to find an envelope containing a DVD and a note from a man named Stuart Coxe, a producer at CBC-TV. His note invited me to call him after watching the DVD.

The disk contained an episode of the BBC-TV *Dragons' Den,* which, as I write this, has been produced in more than thirty countries around the world; the U.S. is the only place where the same concept is given a different name.

I had not heard of *Dragons' Den* before viewing the DVD. I enjoyed watching the show, but the note and the video left me confused. Did they want a cash investment from me? If so, I wasn't interested. The show was entertaining, and I could understand its potential as an audience builder, but I had little interest in backing any show-business venture. The series had yet to air, and while it appeared to be a hit internationally, having been launched in Japan in 2001, there was no assurance it would build an audience in Canada. As a result, when I called Stuart the following day, I may have been a little abrupt. Despite this, Stuart asked if he could drop into my office the following day for a chat, and I agreed to meet with him.

The meeting appeared to go nowhere for the first several minutes. We discussed various things about the show, about my business and about me personally. I had no idea where the session was heading until Stuart smiled and said, "We want you to be one of the Dragons on the show."

That was a switch. They didn't want my money—they wanted *me.* I was going to be a television performer. Boy, wait till my kids hear about this!

Later, I learned a little of the jargon in the television and entertainment industry. Saying "We want you" does not mean "You've got the job!" It merely means you have been invited to an audition, except nobody uses that word. I was just told where and when to arrive for a taping session.

I'm a fairly confident guy, but being ushered into the television studio, with its bank of lights, multiple cameras, a small crowd of businesslike people and the knowledge that I had to prove myself at something I had never attempted before, made me unusually nervous. And it showed. I had worked in television several years before, but this was different. Instead of working behind the scenes, I would be in the spotlight and expected to display my business sense, my perception, my negotiation techniques and my personality, all without script or direction.

During the taping session I assumed I should act iike Robert Herjavec, or at least like somebody playing me, and I was wrong. This sounds a little convoluted, I know, but it simply proves the show-business axiom that the most difficult role to play on stage or on camera is yourself. I was trying to be the perfect Robert Herjavec as he existed in my imagination—incisive, witty, intelligent, polite, overflowing with business ability, all of that. And I was terrible at it.

During breaks in the audition, I could hear mutterings from the corner where the producers of the show were gathered. The words were not encouraging. In the opinion of most producers, I was definitely not the guy to fill the role of the fifth dragon.

Stuart Coxe disagreed with the others. He stopped the action, walked me to a far end of the studio and did his best to praise me, an approach that was really designed to keep my spirits up. Then he added, "Robert, please remember that this is entertainment TV, it is not business." In other words, I should stop trying to be the perfectly logical businessman and relax a little. I was also looking at the camera too often, concerned that I was positioned correctly or responding in the right manner.

Stuart set me straight. "We have fifteen cameras in the studio," he explained. "It's our responsibility to make you look good, and we will. Don't worry about it."

When the second part of the audition began, I grew more relaxed and forgot about my idea of who and what Robert Herjavec should be.

The first pitcher for his company began his number, and I started asking questions. When he didn't provide an adequate answer, I grew persistent until he turned to me, his eyes narrowed and his voice raised, and barked, "Just be quiet for a sec, okay?"

My response was to point at him and almost shout, "Whoa! Nobody tells me to be quiet!" Then I added, for effect, "Okay, maybe my wife after twenty years of marriage."

From the corner where the producers were gathered, I heard Stuart say, "He's our guy."

The original *Dragons' Den* panel included me, Kevin O'Leary, Jim Treliving, Laurence Lewin, co-founder of the La Senza chain of lingerie stores, and Jennifer Wood, president of Cattle & Company Investments. Jennifer departed after the first season, Laurence after the second. Laurence's and Jennifer's chairs were filled by Arlene Dickinson and Brett Wilson.

Abrasive, or Just Honest? Only Kevin Knows for Sure

The most controversial panellist on *Dragons' Den* is Kevin O'Leary. It's interesting that, among those on *Dragons' Den*, he and I were selected to participate in ABC-TV's version of the show, *Shark Tank*, because it's difficult to come up with more contrasting personalities than Kevin's and mine.

In the summer of 2009, both Kevin and I were staying in the same Los Angeles hotel with our families for the first taping of *Shark Tank*. Among all the activity and distractions of that week, I misplaced my room key, and went to the hotel's front desk for a replacement. Following the hotel's correct procedure, the clerk told me he couldn't provide a key without some identification, a policy that makes sense to me. My response was to head to the pool area, where Diane was relaxing with the children, and use her key to enter our room. Not a big deal.

That same week, Kevin lost his room key and asked for a replacement at the front desk, where the clerk repeated what he'd told me—he couldn't issue a new key without some identification.

Kevin's response was to glare at the clerk and say, in a contemptuous manner, "Do you not know who I am? I have been here for a week now. I have talked to you every day. I *demand* that you give me the goddamn room key!"

I'll confess that part of me wants to be Kevin sometimes. Who wouldn't? But I can't shout, "Screw you—give me that key!" It's just not in me.

There have been times when Kevin and I have gotten along well off camera, sharing tales and opinions, just hanging out together.

There have been clashes on camera as well, including one on *Shark Tank* when Kevin lectured a man pitching a deal about his background, which included declaring bankruptcy.

"You're radioactive," Kevin sneered at the man. "No bank will ever touch you in your lifetime."

I had already declared myself out of the deal for various reasons, but Kevin's attitude really irked me. "Why would you say that to him?" I asked Kevin. "Think about it: the guy has a wife and kids at home, and you just called him radioactive."

Kevin's response was immediate and dismissive of me. "He's useless," he said. "He'll never get anybody to loan him money again!"

I tried to explain that we were dealing with a human being, and that nobody in life was radioactive, nobody could be considered a total write-off the way Kevin was describing him.

This disturbed Kevin even more. "The guy went bankrupt," he almost shouted at me. "He's a loser at business."

Everybody fails, I reminded Kevin. The measure of success is not that you fail, but how you get up after you've been knocked down.

"That's a bunch of crap," Kevin replied. "Let me ask you something. Did you give him a dollar? No, you didn't. I'm just more honest than everybody else."

I'm not sure that he is. He is certainly more abrasive than anybody else, a quality that Kevin enjoys displaying.

Our exchange aired on U.S. network TV and probably made a lot of people sit up and take notice of the show. The last word may have come later in the show from the man Kevin labelled radioactive. "I don't know why he was so harsh with me," he said. "I believe everybody in America deserves a second chance."

I buy that belief 100 per cent. Kevin apparently doesn't.

Kevin is correct on one point, and that's our need to tell the truth to those who pitch their ideas on the shows. Most, we suspect, have been encouraged in their ideas by family and friends no matter how outrageous or unmarketable their business proposal may be. These people desperately want to believe they have the Million-Dollar Idea, the magic means of changing their lives completely. Unfortunately, they ignore the fact that others find it easier to lie and encourage them than to tell the truth. In some cases, the lies their friends have told them have led these potential entrepreneurs to spend tens—even hundreds—of thousands of dollars on something that has no hope of commercial success. We tell them the truth. It's often hard to hear, but it is absolutely necessary.

Among the most upsetting events on *Dragons' Den* occur when we discover that the pitchers have already sunk hundreds of thousands of dollars, and sometimes millions, of their personal wealth into a hopelessly doomed venture. Heavily mortgaged family homes and depleted retirement savings are often the only product of these dreams, sometimes pursued over the course of several years.

I understand the passion that drives people to make these decisions, and I applaud it, but only when it's blended with a sense of reality. Having invested years of work and substantial amounts of money in an idea that has yet to prove itself, these people find it difficult to walk away and write off their efforts and investments. It's painful, I know. But continuing to flog an idea that has no hope of succeeding won't wipe the pain away.

Sometimes you need another person to convince you to let go of a bad situation. Along with helping pitchers with good concepts and clear vision succeed, our task involves doing just that: persuading people that they tried and failed, and now it's time to walk away.

But it's never easy, for them or for us.

4

Put Yourself in the Investor's Shoes

The activities behind the scenes of *Dragons' Den* are just as fascinating and dramatic as the action that appears on your television screen.

For example, it takes twenty days to shoot an entire season of *Dragons' Den*, and they are long days—from very early in the morning to very late at night. For the first day or two of each taping session, I'm constantly aware of other places I could be and other things I could be doing, but eventually I fall into the atmosphere and rhythm of the studio, and the "real world" no longer exists. Reality becomes that single large room with crowds of whispering people, clusters of lights, a dozen or more television cameras, and an apparently endless line of people, some desperate and some arrogant, attempting to convince us to fund their dreams with our cash.

Their appearance represents the end of a long journey. Being selected to make their pitch in itself represents success of sorts. Thousands apply each year to appear on *Dragons' Den*. Between

250 and 300 are chosen as pitchers, and barely a quarter of their appearances actually appear on telecasts of the show. What criteria do the producers use to make their choices? The applicants need at least one of two qualities: an exceptional business idea that will grab the attention of the viewing public, or an exceptional personality or other tale that will do the same thing on a different level.

Dragons' Den is not produced for businesspeople. It is produced to capture the attention and loyalty of a broad cross-section of viewers, the same people who also choose to watch *The Simpsons, Antiques Roadshow* and *CSI* on other evenings and at other times. On one occasion, the senior producer of the show, Lisa Gabriele, was giving a speech and the audience challenged her about the authenticity of the show. She responded, "*Dragon's Den* is a TV show that happens to be about business, and not a business show that happens to be on TV." I have always loved that very subtle, but important, distinction.

We are provided with no clue about whom we will see or what they will be pitching, so every response by the panel is immediate and spontaneous. Any expression of impatience or flash of anger between us is genuine, although we may joke about it later. Nothing is pre-scripted and nothing is anticipated.

This makes the environment of the show very unlike the real world, as far as investment decisions are concerned. Outside the studio, the rest of the Dragons and I would take the time to become acquainted with the people seeking our money and determine whether their ideas were valid or not. On *Dragons' Den*, these actions are taken *after* our decision to do a deal, as part of the due-diligence responsibility. As a result, we often find our-selves backtracking, like the time I grew enthusiastic about one pitcher's product that appeared to be the first and only of its kind. Later, I learned the product was based on old technology and at least twenty similar products were already on the market. I didn't lose any investment money, but I wasted a good deal of time.

The production process of the shows represents a challenge for the panel. Those long ten- and twelve-hour days in the studio take their toll, especially on people like us who are accustomed to a dynamic environment where we are obligated to make snap deci-sions, give instructions, measure returns and generally dominate our domain. By the time we've sat through the first dozen or so pitches, one of two things occurs. Either we tend to become leth-argic about making decision, thinking "I'll let Kevin (or Arlene or Brett) do the deal on this one," or we become testy with each other, leading to flashes of anger and even a little name-calling. The first is deadly to good television; the second is invaluable. In fact, sometimes I almost believe the producers extend the shoot-ing days just to raise the irritability factor, with the expectation that we'll begin snapping at each other and increase the drama. And sometimes it works.

The real magic of the shows occurs during the editing process, when the lethargy is eliminated and the energy is emphasized. Although most pitches appear to be made, explained, discussed and evaluated within a few minutes during an actual show, some require more than an hour to complete. As many as ten hours of presentations must be edited down to forty-five minutes, to which commercials, "teasers" for next week's show and other elements are added to make a one-hour show. To do this seamlessly and hold the audience's attention for the entire episode demands a special skill, and I believe both shows are fortunate to have such gifted talent doing the sound and video editing.

Some viewers are curious about how much money we Dragons are paid for an entire season. It's not nearly as much as most people think, and, on an hourly basis, far less than any of us could earn if we dedicated the same number of hours spent in the studio to our full-time businesses. Jim Treliving, Kevin O'Leary and Arlene Dickinson can all benefit to some degree from the national exposure because they deal in consumer products—pizza for Jim, mutual funds for Kevin and marketing expertise for Arlene. Brett and I benefit less. I doubt that The Herjavec Group has earned one extra dollar of profit as a direct result of my appearance on the show.

Will any of us make substantial amounts of profit from the investments we make on the show? It's difficult to say. We agree that our primary objective is to earn back our money, perhaps with a small gain here and there, but none of us expects to add a major lump of cash to our net worth. When someone asks me if I'll make a decent profit on any of the deals, I tell them to ask me again in five years.

Exceptions occur. On an episode of *Shark Tank* broadcast in early 2010, Barbara Corcoran and I invested $40,000 in Grease Monkey Wipes, a business launched and managed by a young man and young woman. The company sold packaged non-toxic wipes that removed grease, oil, tar and other materials from skin and clothing. The product worked, the packaging was great and the two founders were full of talent and ambition, which especially impressed Barbara and me.

Within twenty-four hours of the episode's broadcast, traffic on the Grease Monkey website increased by 4,500 per cent (the site actually crashed from overload) and more orders had been received since the business was launched. This one's a sure winner.

Still, there are no guarantees that we'll see any of the money we invest. So, what keeps me and the others on the show? Each of the others has his or her own reasons. At the risk of sounding corny, mine is the way it inspires people to at least explore the idea of creating their own business and pursue a dream of wealth and independence. I couldn't begin to count the number of people who have told me that the show inspires them, even when pitchers leave empty-handed. When it comes to realizing their full potential in life, too many people give in to inertia until they witness someone else who has taken at least the first steps towards their dream. I like that. I especially like the idea that someone, years from now, will be congratulated on his or her success and perhaps respond that *Dragons' Den* inspired them to go for it.

Tempted Back by Kevin O'Leary

I'll admit I enjoyed my new status as something of a celebrity. Most people with even an average ego would get the same satisfaction out of weekly appearances on network television. By the end of the second season of *Dragons' Den*, however, I began resenting the amount of time the show was taking from my business activities and informed the producers I would not be doing a third season.

After much searching and auditioning, the producers of *Dragons'*
Den settled on Brett Wilson as my replacement. Then, a few weeks
before taping for Season Three was to begin, they were informed
that Laurence Lewin had been diagnosed with terminal cancer, and
a second replacement would have to be located.

More auditions followed without a decision being made.
Barely a week before taping was to begin, Kevin O'Leary called
me. "The show sucks without you," he said. "You have to come
back!" Stuart Coxe added his plea to sentimental Kevin's, and I
agreed to return.

At one point, I asked the producers why they had such apparent difficulty replacing me. Hadn't they auditioned dozens of
prospects? "Sure," one of them said. "We found people smarter
than you, wealthier than you, better looking than you and more
charming than you. But when we put them on camera, they just
didn't work as well as you do."

I'm not sure if my ego was stroked or bruised by their comments, but I haven't regretted coming back.

It took a year or so to build a following, but by the end of 2009
Dragons' Den could boast an average of more than two million
viewers per show—meaning we attract more viewers than *Hockey*
Night in Canada.

Incidentally, the two questions most asked by fans of the
Dragons' Den are "Is Kevin O'Leary really that mean?" and "Does
Robert Herjavec wear coloured contact lenses?" The answers are
yes and no.

Things That People Do Well When Pitching a Deal

Engage us quickly. Anybody who has our total attention for the first thirty seconds probably doubles the chance of getting a deal.

Maintain a pleasant demeanour. Knowing how to be persuasive without being pushy is a gift. Those who have it attract our attention.

Bring us a great idea—one that's original and appeals to a defined market.

Know how to make a good presentation. Backing up their pitch with solid facts and figures, delivered in a confident manner, helps their cause immensely.

Have recorded actual sales or have a realistic plan to generate them. Nothing succeeds like real sales.

Submit a reasonable valuation of their idea or company. It doesn't pay to be greedy.

Things That People Do Badly

Fail to be honest. It makes no sense to exaggerate success because not a penny will be spent until due diligence is completed.

Don't know their market. Wise investors don't put their money into things they don't understand—or, worse, things the person seeking their money doesn't understand.

Have recorded no sales.

Are unrealistic about growth. There are many overnight successes in fairy tales and movies, and very few in real life.

Become rude. You don't have to be kissy-face. Just be pleasant.

Use sex. Attractive people have succeeded, but only if their pitch has worked in other ways as well. But the woman who dressed her daughter in a skimpy bikini to get our attention assured herself that she wouldn't get my money. What does it say about someone who would use her own child that way? Not much.

5

How to Pitch a Good Idea—
and How Not To

I'll admit that I was excited at being invited, along with Kevin O'Leary, to play the same role on *Shark Tank* as I had been playing on *Dragons' Den*. The prospect was terrific, especially the ego-boosting thought that *Shark Tank* could deliver an audience ten times the size of *Dragons' Den*. The fact that it would be produced by Mark Burnett, who practically invented reality television, in Hollywood, California, sparked my enthusiasm even more.

When Burnett gave me the official word that I would indeed be part of the American version of a show that was already a global hit in more than a dozen countries, I happened to be skiing with my son at Big White in Kelowna, B.C. I spent the next day or two faxing contracts and other paperwork back and forth between Kelowna and Hollywood, telling myself that the kid from Croatia had made it—a major U.S. network television show!

Just as my son Brendan and I were about to return to Toronto, reality arrived with a thud in a telephone call from one of the executive producers. "We really want you to do the show," the producer said, "but we're bringing in another shark."

How could my Hollywood career crash before it got off the ground? It involved the little matter of a visa. Without one, I couldn't open my mouth in a U.S. production. *Shark Tank* began shooting in less than a week, and all the lawyers and immigration specialists I'd consulted had assured me it was impossible to snare a U.S. O-1 visa, issued for "extraordinary talent"—that sound you hear in the background is my wife laughing at the description— in such a short period of time. Totally unheard of, I was informed.

Apparently, no one informed Burnett. He obtained a O-1 visa for me within twenty-four hours, and off I went to Hollywood. What does that tell you about the power of the combined forces of Sony (who own the worldwide rights to the show's concept), ABC-TV and Disney?

The night before shooting the pilot, we all gathered in a Los Angeles restaurant for dinner together—the Sharks and the whole executive production group led by Mark Burnett. We were all having a fine time until, halfway through the evening, Mark stood up and announced he was leaving for home. "You may have noticed," he said, "that we have six Sharks here tonight, but we only need five for the show. So one of you will be going home tomorrow at ten in the morning. Cheers!" And he was off.

The rest of the dinner that evening was very quiet.

When taping started the next morning, I held nothing back, and it paid off. I was named one of the five Sharks, and the pilot proved so successful that it became the show's initial episode, which is highly unusual.

Playing the same role in both countries gives me an opportunity to compare how people on each side of the border deal with television.

The stakes are much higher on U.S. than on Canadian television, if only because the U.S. audience is ten times bigger. Large audiences generate large revenues, which mean bigger stakes for the producers, the network and the panellists. As a result, there is substantially more pressure to score a major hit quickly. It took four years for *Dragons' Den* to achieve hit status in Canada, but there was no way we would have that much time to make a hit with *Shark Tank*.

The pressure also leads to more scripting and less ad-libbing in the U.S. version. Talking off the top of your head too much can waste time or leave the wrong impression. That's one reason why *Shark Tank* uses pre-produced introductions for many pitchers, with lots of explanation regarding their background and the nature of their idea or business before they appear in front of the Sharks. In Canada, it's left to the audience to absorb the same information as the Dragons receive, and at the same time.

In other instances, no real difference exists between Canada and the U.S., nor, I suspect, can one be found among the dozen other regions where the show is produced and aired. A universal desire exists among people to do more for themselves and their families, and to elevate themselves in various ways—material, social, cultural and more. It drives entrepreneurs everywhere, in and out of the TV studios.

Sometimes the Pitchers Bite Back

One mark of a driven and potentially successful pitcher on *Dragons' Den* is the ability to negotiate in front of the cameras and come up with a deal that's good for both sides. Pitchers find themselves being dismissed for being unrealistic about the potential value of their business or for not appreciating the concerns of the Dragons about recovering at least their investment, preferably with a reasonable profit. Very few are prepared to counter an offer that's unacceptable to them with a proposal that appears to work for both sides. Only the bright ones succeed.

Jonathan Miller, a *Shark Tank* pitcher, came to the show prepared with facts and attitude, along with a promising product. His energy bars attracted the attention of Kevin Harrington, who offered $150,000 for Miller's entire company plus a 4–percent licensing fee. Miller's response that selling his entire company would "demotivate" him struck a chord with the rest of the Sharks, and Harrington offered the same deal for just 35 per cent of the company plus the licensing arrangement. Miller countered for 25 per cent, leading Harrington to suggest they split the difference at 30 per cent.

The entrepreneur gave up less than a third of his company, secured a licensing arrangement and got access to some badly needed capital. In essence, he was one of the rare Sharks who bit back at us and won. Good for him, although I would not have made an offer as generous as the one made by Kevin Harrington.

Anger and Naïveté, and Sometimes Both

Pitchers in the U.S. are very similar to their Canadian counterparts. Some are brilliant in their presentations, fully equipped to deal with the Dragons' or Sharks' questions about sales, profit potential, market size and so on. Others are hopelessly naive about how to value their business, or what it takes to persuade an investor to part with money. Most are nervous about appearing in front of us, but that's one of the points of the production: we have the money and the spotlight, they have the idea and the need, and they need us far more than we will ever need them.

This may be why pitchers who are turned down and even insulted (usually by Kevin) for their audacity at asking us for money accept the decision mildly. A few exceptions have occurred when unsuccessful pitchers grew angry enough to prompt calls to security staff. The most notable was a man pitching an idea to *Dragons' Den* based on a website that none of us on the panel could understand. The situation was made worse because the pitcher brought a crowd of supporters who clapped and shouted "Believe!" on cue. The more he talked, and the more his gang clapped and shouted, the more we realized he didn't have a website. It was all a sham. We also recognized that he was very arrogant. Everyone making a pitch to Dragons or Sharks has to feel confident, but he was well across the line that separates confidence from arrogance.

When I declared I was out of any deal with him, he claimed he couldn't understand how I could turn him down. "You're just like me!" he said, and I responded that I was not like him and had never been like him, that I never acted so arrogantly.

Leaving the studio, he and his gang grew angry enough for the producers to call security, which led to some pushing and shoving on their way out of the building.

That's the important thing to remember about passion: it's beneficial when it drives you to success; it's not when your plans are foiled.

Five Ways TV Is Like the Real World

1. **You have a short amount of time to make your point.** In real life, you don't know when the other person isn't really listening to you. In the world of television, you always know.
2. **People judge you by who you appear to be.**
3. **Past success does not guarantee future success.** Great audience ratings last year won't save you if your numbers slip this year.
4. **Fast learners have a distinct advantage.**
5. **People who don't really matter love you when you're important, and shun you when you're not important.**

Five Ways TV Is *Not* Like the Real World

1. **Life is long.** TV is short—about forty-five minutes per hour.
2. **Despite your audience size and approval rating, the only opinions that should really matter to you are those of your family and friends.**
3. **Success is not measured by the hour.** It is measured in years.
4. **In the real world, you cannot be called a major success based on two consecutive weeks of good ratings.**
5. **People who truly love you do so no matter how low your audience ratings are.**

6

Why Pitches Go Wrong

If you have watched *Dragons' Den,* you realize why it has achieved success as a prime-time entertainment vehicle. Within the human drama of this program is a message that everyone can absorb concerning ambition and the difference between success and failure.

The show also represents an informative and revealing peek into the personalities of businesspeople who have the inclination, if not the determination, to succeed on their own, perhaps with some investment assistance from us Dragons. What I find missing in many of them is the sense that they are driven to succeed. Ambitious, hopeful and energetic, yes. The ones who are truly driven, however, demonstrate more than that. They bring a sense of energy and conviction with them that is almost boiling over as soon as they enter the studio.

I can tell within the first thirty seconds whether I am likely to entrust my money to the individual making the pitch, even before

I hear a description of the business needing investment. It's not just nervousness; it's something intangible: a blend of confidence, assurance and even a bit of swagger. When we see it, we know we are dealing with someone driven to succeed; when it's not present, we become less confident about the entire deal. If the first impression fails to make me confident, the pitchers have sixty seconds to change my mind. If I'm not sold by then, I'm out.

A New York University study[1] tracked the success/failure rate of new companies over a seven-year period and also tracked the actual returns earned by venture capitalists across an extended period of time. The study was prepared in 2007, just before the severe recession struck in March 2008, and the returns were generated by surviving companies, factoring in losses as a result of companies that failed to endure over the same periods would drastically reduce the levels of return.

So how did they do?

Start-up investors made the greatest gains, which is understandable since they took the biggest risk, but only after ten years had passed. By that point, the surviving companies returned about 33 per cent annually, justifying the risk. Even after twenty years, these in-at-the-beginning investors were banking earnings of more than 21 per cent each year. Late-stage investors cut their risks and their profits, bringing in 8.5 per cent annually after ten years and 14.5 per cent twenty years after start-up. They did better earlier in the game, however: five years

---

1 Aswath Damodaran, "Valuing Young, Start-up and Growth Companies: Estimation Issues and Valuation Challenges," Stern School of Business, New York University, 2009.

after the launch of a company start-up, investors were returning 5 per cent annually while their late-stage colleagues more than doubled that return.

Returns like these are money magnets to Dragons, but we are also anchored in realism. Dramatic strike-it-rich investments are rare on the show, just as they are in real life, but they occur. Reggae Reggae Sauce, a bottled hot condiment that its creator launched with an investment of £50,000 from the UK version of *Dragons' Den*, was a major winner. Supermarkets across Britain and Ireland reportedly sell fifty thousand bottles each week. At £1.50 (about $2.40 Canadian), both the entrepreneur and the *Dragons' Den* investors are pocketing healthy earnings.

The Most Common Mistake by Pitchers: Being Greedy

Kevin O'Leary claims that pitchers on *Dragons' Den* who over-value their companies are greedy. I prefer to take a more charitable view. I believe most of them are floating on a cloud of optimism and enthusiasm while having no concept of the way businesses are valued in the cold, hard world of investors—who, of course, have been accused of being a little greedy and rapacious on their own.

I don't know whether to laugh, cry or get angry when someone arrives for a taping of either show with a business concept valued at $1 million even though it has yet to make a penny in sales. Dreams and expectations are wonderful things, but you cannot cash them at a bank or even trade one for a cup of coffee. The only criteria that count in business are sales and profits.

Greed combined with a lack of understanding of basic business principles has destroyed many dreams of pitchers on *Dragons' Den*. I especially recall the father-and-son team who had created and patented a hinge for a functional folding guitar. The hinge would be located where the neck meets the body of the guitar, the part of the instrument that is vulnerable when it's being transported. The hinge worked; folding and unfolding the neck actually kept the instrument in tune, a fact that Kevin O'Leary confirmed by demonstrating his finger-picking guitar style to the world.

Creating the hinge was a brilliant idea, but the pitch the two men made on *Shark Tank* was not nearly as clever. They wanted $500,000 for a 5-per-cent stake in a company that would have the exclusive right to produce guitars with the feature, an outrageous valuation of $10 million for a company that had yet to make a sale. To everyone except the inventors, the wisest move would have been to license the patent for existing manufacturers that would offer the same feature. The two Kevins, Herrington and O'Leary, offered $500,000 for 51 per cent of the company holding the patent, plus assistance in producing a television promotion and negotiating the best licensing arrangement.

The inventors rejected the idea, which could have put millions of dollars in their pockets within a few years. Instead, they'll have to find financing from other sources and perhaps engage in negotiations with guitar makers on their own. Independence is a wonderful thing, but it's best enjoyed in the right place and under the right conditions. In my opinion, you can buy a lot of independence with several million dollars in cash and future royalties.

I became involved in a similar situation with a man who Robert Allison, whose Lifebelt product prevented a car from starting until the driver's seatbelt was properly connected. I appreciated that Robert appeared to be driven by the opportunity to save lives, which would surely occur if every vehicle on the road were equipped with a Lifebelt. The best way to do this, in my opinion, was to secure a licensing deal with as many automobile manufacturers as quickly as possible, a mission Kevin O'Leary was prepared to undertake if the inventor would sell him the patent for $500,000. I considered Kevin's offer drastically underpriced, so I upped the offer to a million dollars for the same deal, which didn't endear me to Kevin but didn't impress Robert Allison either—he turned me down.

I expected Allison to come back with a counter-offer, one that would generate royalties in perpetuity. Depending on the royalty and sales levels, he could have netted $100,000 annually and still have a million dollars in the bank just for putting his signature to the deal. He preferred to use his idea as the basis for his own business. I understand and respect his thinking, but I do not agree with it.

Robert Allison was driven to become a business owner, and that's fine. Unfortunately, I think he was too emotionally involved in attaining that identity, and it clouded his ability to see my proposal, perhaps with some negotiated tweaking, as a better business deal. He failed to realize that you can come up with new ideas faster than you can build a successful business, and Allison is basically an ideas kind of guy.

He missed two more hard-nosed facts. The first is that successful entrepreneurs treat businesses like commodities—or, in a slightly different analogy, like farmers raising crops. You buy or plant the business, you grow it until the price is right, and you sell it to the highest bidder. You don't become emotionally involved with it as an entity, even to the point of calling it your "baby," as I warned about earlier.

The second fact he ignored is that very few businesspeople hit a home run in their first time at bat. Even fewer do it without a business partner who understands the game and has the interest and wherewithal to help them score big. Allison may prove to be an exception; but each day that passes is one day less for him to enjoy the benefits he could have earned through the cash infusion, licensing strategy and royalties he might have earned with my deal.

We often hear that a valuation is at least partially based on previous investments made by friends or relatives, people who delight in "getting in on the ground floor" with their brother-in-law or cousin. I think believing in blood relatives is a wonderful attitude, but it's usually a terrible business decision.

If the guidelines below enable one pitcher on either show to determine a reasonable valuation for his or her venture, I'll be pleased.

How to Value Your Venture

1. **Your company is worth what the market says it is worth.** Whether your company's bank account is in overdraft or you have a million dollars in cash in your coffers, neither you nor your accountants dictate the current price. Only the market can. This may appear unfair (although it can also prove highly

profitable—overvaluations are not unknown), but that's how the real world works. Many pitchers have walked out of Dragons' Den totally convinced that our valuations of their businesses were wrong. The truth is we are never wrong because, in that particular market, our valuation is the only one that matters.

1. **No sales equal no value.** Limited profit equals limited value. History is filled with superior products handled by competent companies that could neither achieve sufficient sales nor value to survive. Just as the investment market sets the value of your company, the general market determines the success of your product or service. It is cruel, unfair and unfortunately true. People of a certain age recall how videocassettes brought the convenience of movie viewing into homes a generation ago. Two incompatible formats were introduced, and in every respect Sony's Betamax was technologically superior. It didn't matter. The public favoured the competitive format, VHS. Without sales and profits, Sony's technical superiority had little value in the wider consumer market.

2. **An established value can be enhanced.** Assuming your business has recorded a reasonable level of sales and appears to be profitable, its perceived value can be improved through judicious use of comparables and forecasts. Look at similar companies, some of which may be your competitors, and try to get a handle on their size and growth record. Can you make a reasonable case for duplicating their success with the added benefit of a unique improvement in quality or price? Financial forecasts are extremely complex, but you should prepare

figures that are intentionally conservative and realistic and that reflect the reality of the business world. Launching a chain of pet food stores, for example, may prove more likely to succeed than a biotechnology operation, but future profits, if any, will be substantially lower.

7

Believe in Yourself

I arrived in North America as an eight-year-old immigrant kid from Croatia whose father's net worth, by the time we settled in a basement apartment provided by friends, totalled twenty bucks in cash. From that day forward, my life unfolded like the classic "immigrant makes good" tale: teased at school for my poor English and different customs, supported by a father who walked miles each way to a menial job, loved by a mother who believed in her son and encouraged him to pursue his dreams, and determined to justify the sacrifices my parents made for me.

Despite various false starts and detours, I believed that I would reach a level of success and financial reward beyond anything my parents or I could have imagined back in Croatia, which was part of communist Yugoslavia at the time. I hope this doesn't sound arrogant—I dislike arrogance, while I value determination, which is not the same thing at all—but I simply believed I would succeed, and I did. I also accepted the fact that if I did not succeed I would likely wind up in a ditch somewhere, maybe searching for discarded bottles and cans to cash in for their deposit. It was a "shoot the works" attitude, and I was comfortable with it.

Within ten years of graduating from university with a degree in English Literature and a minor in Political Science, I was running my own computer technology–based company. Later, I sold the firm for a substantial amount of cash. Press reports have claimed it was around $100 million and, while that's not accurate, I have never disputed the figure. When you hear amounts like that being thrown around, by the way, you should ask yourself how much the entrepreneur actually pockets in cash. I owned 90 per cent of my firm (employees owned the rest), and that's how much I kept. Others may boast they sold their companies for, let's say, $300 million or more, but unless their ownership was total and the deal was made entirely in cash, that's not the amount they deposited in their bank account.

Since selling my company in the late 1990s I have started more firms, earned more money and learned more lessons. Only a few of those lessons have had anything to do with the curricula of business schools and the discipline of MBA guidelines; almost all of them are linked to a simple, universal trait found—to a widely ranging degree—in all human beings: the ability to imagine a goal, and believe in the likelihood of reaching it.

Other issues are involved, of course. These include a knack for being able to see just far enough into the future—not too soon, not too distant—to recognize opportunity before others see it. Another essential ingredient is the determination to handle obstacles encountered on the road to success, either by destroying them completely or simply walking around them. As time passed,

I also realized that large-scale success can only be achieved with the support of a team whose members share the same vision and willpower as their leader.

The Odds Are Against You—So What?

It's easy to find a reason for not trying to become successful in business. You may tell yourself you lack formal education, social standing, contacts among influential people or sufficient start-up capital, or come up with a dozen other reasons to abandon the idea. In contrast, you need only one reason to succeed, and that's the conviction that you are capable of doing it.

Everybody who launches a new business, especially one that deals with a unique service or product, encounters people with reasons why they will fail. They have good reason: statistics record that the majority of start-up companies fail within three years— just so you know that the odds are against you.

The fact is, anybody can name multiple reasons why a new business will fail, but the business needs only one good reason for it to succeed. If you know that reason, and are prepared to work hard enough to prove you're right, you'll ignore the naysayers.

An economics student at Yale University named Fred Smith did this in 1962. Smith submitted a new business concept as the basis for an undergraduate term paper. His professor grudgingly gave him a grade of C for his work and suggested that his next business idea be a little more practical and realistic. After graduating with a bachelor's degree and spending six years in the military, Smith founded a company based on his paper. That company was FedEx.

Everybody will offer you free advice, but the only good thing about free advice is the price. No one will know what you are going through to succeed in your business except you. No one will believe in the idea as strongly as you, because, if they did, they would launch it on their own. And no one will experience the extreme emotions of both success and setbacks, because they're not as driven to fulfill their dream as you.

It all begins with belief. Without enough belief in yourself and your goal, you may as well stay on square one—or, better still, step aside and let someone else take your place. I respect people who choose the comfort and security of a good job with a large and prosperous employer who offers a good salary and a healthy benefits package. Most of them work hard, achieve some level of satisfaction, provide comfort and security for their family, and retire to play golf and spend a few weeks in Florida each winter.

It's very nice. But it's not for me. Maybe it never was.

There is a difference between me—and the other panellists on *Dragons' Den*—and those who prefer a salaried job while climbing the corporate ladder. The difference varies and is very difficult to define, but it exists nevertheless.

It's easy to look at all the current and past judges on *Dragons' Den* and assume that the only thing that separates us from the viewers is the amount of money each of us has. That's true, to a point. Many of our personal values are the same as the majority of the television audience watching us. We value our families, love our children, believe in freedom and decency and all of that. But something exists among us that we don't share with many other people, and it's easier to describe than name, so I won't attempt to hang a label on it. Perhaps you can, when you learn a little more about me and about the other Dragons.

In some ways, I have more in common with Kevin O'Leary, whose personality is 180 degrees from my own, than with a young man or woman in search of a job that promises little more than an adequate salary and a reasonable assurance of permanent employment. Kevin and I have something in us that many others lack, and it can be found in others on *Dragons' Den.*

I've already mentioned Jim Treliving's background as an RCMP officer who abandoned his career to launch a chain of restaurants across North America. Did Jim's experience as a Mountie prepare him to become one of the most successful food-service franchisers in the industry? It's difficult to see how. Something else drove him to abandon his childhood dream in favour of risking it all as an entrepreneur. Incidentally, Jim conducts himself with quiet focus on his work and on the people he meets, but I would not want to meet an angry Jim Treliving in a dark alley.

Jennifer Wood, a Dragon on the first year of the show, owned and managed ten thousand head of cattle and would have been perfectly at home in a John Wayne western movie, riding a horse and chasing errant cattle across the prairie. Is she your image of an entrepreneur? Probably not, yet she shared the same drive as the rest of us. And how do you explain Laurence Lewin, who travelled to Montreal from England to set up a computer system, then switched to women's fashions with the launch of La Senza? Every day, millions of women from Canada to Australia slip into La Senza's bras, panties and chemises, purchased at one of more than seven hundred stores worldwide. (Laurence had a wonderfully dry sense of humour. He once turned to be me and said, "Robert, I know more about women's knickers than anybody else in the entire world!") How does a proper English gentleman with training as a computer programmer achieve such astonishing success marketing lingerie? It was obviously not through formal education. Sadly, Laurence passed away following the first two seasons of *Dragons' Den.*

Arlene Dickinson, who replaced Jennifer after the first season of *Dragons' Den,* built Venture Communications into a strategic and creative marketing powerhouse for clients such as Toyota, Unilever, Forzani Group and others. Nobody intimidates Arlene, nor should they, based on her understanding of marketing principles and strategies. Brett Wilson, an all-around good guy who supports a wide range of charitable causes, is just as effective at making complex business and investment decisions as any of us.

The Sharks on the ABC-TV show with whom Kevin O'Leary and I share the studio have the same inner strength. Barbara Corcoran is tough as nails and is the only person in history to successfully countersue Donald Trump over a lost sales commission. Each year on the anniversary of that victory, she sends Trump a dozen roses to remind him about it, a gesture I'm almost certain is not entirely welcomed by The Donald.

Daymond John of *Shark Tank* is one of my favourite people anywhere. He's lots of fun to be around, but his jokes and big smile hide a determination as steely as any I've encountered. How else would you describe a guy who once supported himself by dancing in Times Square for nickels, sold T-shirts out of the back of his car, and is now a guy who sets the tastes and standards for urban clothing in the USA and ultimately around the world?

The last shark, Kevin Harrington, operates in the realm of infomercials, a world that is uniquely American and one that I don't fully grasp. But Kevin not only understands that business, he dominates it in a "take no prisoners" manner.

Why us? What qualified us for the degree of success we've achieved?

The most obvious answer is that we were driven to go beyond the level of satisfaction others might have settled for. Daymond, I'm sure, wasn't the only person to dance for money in Times Square, and many people have baked and sold pizzas without coming close to achieving the success of Jim Treliving.

Did pure luck make the difference? Is it because we all happened to be doing the right thing in the right place at the right time? Luck plays a role in everything, but anyone who attributes success to good fortune alone is not facing facts.

I'm not sure any of us was fulfilling a childhood dream of achieving wealth through business ventures. I didn't operate a lemonade stand with dreams of franchising as a seven-year-old, nor did I throw my university diploma aside on the way home from graduation, intent on incorporating my first company. In fact, I launched my first wholly owned firm because I *had* to, not because I planned to.

But that choice—the one that involved risk and vision and sacrifice—was the same one that every other panel member on *Dragons' Den* has made at some time in their lives, and it was a decision that most people choose to avoid. Is it all in the genes? Maybe that explains the difference. John Gartner, a psychiatry professor at Johns Hopkins University medical school, conducted research that supports this idea. In his book *The Hypomanic Edge: The Link Between (a Little) Craziness and (a Lot of) Success in America,* Gartner suggests that successful entrepreneurs suffer from hypomania, which he describes as a psychological condition—marked by high energy and boundless self-confidence—falling just short of bipolar disease, also known as a manic-depressive state. Unlike people suffering from bipolar disorders, those with hypomania rarely collapse into suicidal despair. Instead, after suffering a major negative event in their life, they pick themselves up and resume their battle as confident as ever.

I like that description of "high energy and boundless self-confidence." I also like the findings of other researchers on the same topic who have suggested that becoming, or desiring to become, a successful entrepreneur may be embedded in a person's DNA. This sounds a little far-fetched until you consider that during the Middle Ages something drove a few risk-takers beyond their country's borders in search of wealth and fame. It wasn't always a need for arable ground; it was usually a hunger to build something that had never existed before. What inspired Marco Polo, Columbus and hundreds of other intrepid souls to risk everything in search of new opportunity? It wasn't just curiosity, and I don't think the prize attraction was money, either. I suspect it was an urge to create something new, something nobody had explored before as a business enterprise.

Some researchers attribute this attitude to a migratory gene passed among descendants. They suggest that immigrants to America, who left their native countries behind to take risks in a society they knew nothing about, carried the gene, and it became common among Americans after a few generations.

I'm not sure of the validity of this argument, but it may confirm my suspicion that the urge to start and operate your own company really is "in the blood" and not just a wild desire to become wealthy.

Another aspect of being a driven entrepreneur is something I like to call "a tolerance for ambiguity," which among other things explains why people like me often have messy desks. (Beware of accountants with messy desks. Ambiguity in an accountant is not necessarily a desirable quality.) The untidiness isn't always the result of running here and there. It reflects the knack of seeing opportunities all around us, some of which are acted upon while others are merely evaluated. Which explains the reference to ambiguity.

Five Commandments for Budding Businesspeople

1. **Identify your passion.** People start businesses for one of two reasons: to make "a quick buck" or to fulfill a passion of being independent and perhaps building a substantial corporation. Passion keeps you going when others, who may doubt your ability, are attending parties, watching television or sleeping.

2. **Do your research.** Having a great idea is not sufficient reason alone to start a company. You must identify and quantify a real need. While you're at it, you should determine who your competitors are and whether it is wise to challenge them for the same dollar.

3. **Hold off on expansion.** Early successes may launch even bigger dreams. Ignore them in the beginning; starting small

enables you to more effectively deal with problems (and problems are inevitable). Remaining small also enables you to change the focus of your business if necessary. Consider expansion only when your core business is running smoothly and profitably, and your assets permit you to fund the growth.

4. **Set fixed goals.** Write down no more than five or six goals for your business and consult them on a regular basis. Operating your business involves making so many decisions that you may feel overwhelmed at times. Reviewing your goals enables you to prioritize what must be done and when; if the problems do not relate directly to your goals, their importance is diminished, along with their urgency.

5. **Have an exit strategy.** This may seem inappropriate at the planning stage, but it can guide the way you grow and shape your company. Do you plan to sell it for a capital gain? Share management duties when it reaches a defined size? Close the doors and walk away at some point? Leave it for your children, assuming they are both capable and interested? Each alternative may influence your operating decisions differently.

8

Having One Good Idea Is Never Enough

Most people assume that one good idea, one inspiration unlike any other, is all they need to achieve success. Somewhere, they suspect, a million-dollar concept waits for them to find it, as though the core of becoming an entrepreneur lurks in a winning lottery ticket filed in the back of their mind.

It's never as simple as that. Good ideas are like mushrooms: they may thrive in the dark of your mind and imagination, but at some point they have to be brought into the light of the real world—and, to my knowledge, nobody ever paid a million dollars for a mushroom.

Forget about mushrooms. How about mousetraps? The American philosopher Ralph Waldo Emerson supposedly advised, "Build a better mousetrap and the world will beat a path to your door." His comment sent untold thousands of people to their workshops, where they began designing a better mousetrap or egg beater or garbage pail or some other revolutionary device, dreaming of wealth and glory that never arrived.

On *Dragons' Den*, we've seen almost every imaginable variation of the better mousetrap idea. I especially remember the fake
golf club with a hollow shaft that men could pee into while halfway through a game (and far from the clubhouse). Others were
just as original and impractical. Every pitcher we encountered
honestly believed that he or she had created the better mousetrap
Emerson talked about.

Emerson wasn't entirely correct. If the world doesn't know
about your better mousetrap or believe it's an improvement or
know where your workshop door is, it won't beat a path anywhere. If your mousetrap works twice as well as others, but costs
three times as much, they may beat that path to your door but
they won't open their wallets. And more to the point, maybe
they don't have a mouse problem at all. Or maybe they *like* mice.
Or maybe . . .

Not every fortune is made from an original idea alone. Some of
the biggest successes in business were the result of taking a proven
idea and massaging it a little to make it more attractive or more
profitable. McDonald's defined the fast-food concept many years
before Dave Thomas launched Wendy's, yet Thomas managed to
build a billion-dollar empire by doing things his way. And Michael
Dell had little to do with the concept of personal computers, yet
he made billions of dollars by finding a new way to market them.
Neither Thomas nor Dell originated the concepts behind their
businesses. They originated a new way of exploiting an existing
concept, and they did it better than others.

People who believe their fortunes will be made from a clever
idea alone are like missionaries, determined to spread the word

about their invention or their ingenuity to the world, which they believe will reward them with enormous riches and fulfill their dreams. Whenever I encounter people like them on *Dragons' Den*, I want to remind them that missionaries were often people who harboured a dream of being welcomed as saviours and ended up being burnt at the stake or suffering some other ignominious (not to say unexpected) fate.

The world is not waiting to hand over money for a better mousetrap, or a better anything, just because it appears to be a good idea. The world may reward you for a good idea and a lot of hard work—a heck of a lot of hard work—but both of these qualities, in large quantities, guarantee you nothing except a chance at success. More than the flash of a great idea, you need the sweat and skill of proper execution, which involves taking your idea— *any* idea—and executing it better than others.

Feeding Creativity

Here's another difference between successful businesspeople and those who cling to the belief that one good idea will make them a million dollars: creativity. If you lack a creative sense, you may be a highly effective manager, but you will never be a successful entrepreneur.

In one sense, starting a business is as creative as writing a novel or painting a landscape. You create something out of thin air. You often work with intangibles. You begin with no limits to the scope of your imagination and end with a creation that reflects your own unique skills and vision. And you learn to improvise when needed.

Good creativity feeds itself. When you're creating something that fulfills a vision and almost overwhelms your life, you don't need to persuade yourself to get up and go to work each morning. You can hardly wait to leap out of bed when the alarm goes off because you are watching your concept evolve even while you're making it happen.

On another level, your creativity may move you step by step from a home office to rented office space to a suite of offices and perhaps into your own building, crafting your creation along the way, all the while surrounding yourself with people who bring specialized skills to keep the evolution going. They are your support team, and you lead and inspire them. In return, they play a role in the creative act you're performing. It's a symbiotic process. They need your vision and your belief in the inevitability of its success; without those elements, they have no employment. You need their specialized skills and multiple talents; without them, your vision will remain nothing but a dream trapped inside your imagination.

This sounds complicated, I know. You're creative, like any artist. And you're a manager, like some corporate executive. Wait a minute. Are you both? Or are you neither?

I say you're neither. In my view, you're someone whose determination to achieve your goal and prove the validity of your vision generates something that we can all recognize even if we can't easily name it. Some people call it symbiosis, which is too academic for me. "Team spirit" is close, but it sounds like the stuff a high school football coach demands.

For now, let's call it shared enthusiasm. I'm pleased that I've

managed to produce shared enthusiasm in the companies I created, and it was as responsible for the monetary rewards and the
personal satisfaction I enjoyed as any other quality.

Keep Looking Up

Novelists writing books, actors preparing for their roles, musicians crafting songs, poets composing verses, and painters lay-
ing their first brushstroke on a blank canvas have no fixed idea
how their work will look and sound when they complete it. They
know, of course, their intent. The novelist is writing a murder
mystery, the actor is playing the role of a bereaved widow, the
musician is composing a love song, and so on. But throughout
the creative process, they are like someone driving on a strange
road through a heavy fog; they know their destination, but they
can see only a short distance ahead, and they are uncertain about
what lurks around the next corner. Around that corner lie both
inspiration and challenges, and every creative person faces the
latter. Some are created by others, while some occur when creative
people challenge themselves, reaching beyond their grasp.

Only someone who is determined to reach his or her destination despite all obstacles, and who honestly enjoys developing
something out of nothing, will overcome the inevitable challenges. If you believe strongly enough in yourself and your vision,
you'll see these obstacles and challenges in a different way from
others. Many people consider them the end of their dreams, or
perhaps nature's way of telling them they should forget about
being an entrepreneur and settle for a salaried position with
some large, established company. When faced with the cold, hard

facts of launching a business, the true entrepreneur shrugs and assumes they don't apply to his or her situation.

What are these cold, hard facts? A survey conducted by the U.S. Commerce Department a few years ago found that of every ten small businesses launched, seven will survive their first year, three will still be going after three years, and only two will remain after five years. That's eight out of ten businesses collapsing within five years, many of them taking all of their founder's money, not to mention their dreams, with them.

Those who believe in their vision and capabilities don't care. They're different. Nothing will deter them. In explaining this attitude, I ask people to imagine they are walking down the street on a lovely sunny day, when a grand piano being lifted up to the top floor of an apartment building slips out of the ropes holding it and crashes to the sidewalk, landing a few feet in front of them.

The classic response is to panic at the prospect that the piano might have crushed them on impact, or to thank some deity for protecting them from certain death, or to consider legal action against the incompetent fools who let the instrument drop.

The entrepreneur's response? "Gee, that was a nice piano." Danger? Risk? Hazard? Not a big deal. Happens all the time.

Worrying about a piano falling on you as you walk down the street is enough to keep you indoors every day. No one can say it will never happen; you just have to believe it will never happen to *you*, and that's the mindset of people with a true entrepreneurial spirit. Companies go broke every day, which is a lot more frequently than pianos drop from great heights onto pedestrians, but you cannot dwell on that possibility. To succeed in business, you have to do three things: work your butt off, be extravagant with your dreams but practical with your expenses, and avoid thinking about failure.

If you were truly logical and practical, as far as your financial security was concerned, wouldn't you become a plumber or a teacher or some other occupation where a proven demand exists and no risk of capital is involved? Life brings us enough pain, expected and unexpected, deserved and undeserved. Why add more by striking out on your own?

Because somewhere in your personality, you honestly believe that you will avoid the falling pianos.

Just How Hot Is Hell, Anyway?

No one should launch a business before collecting as much information about the process as possible. But you will never gather all the information you need, or plan to handle all the problems you'll encounter. No matter how well prepared you may be, especially when it's your first business launch, you can never foresee all the stumbling blocks, disasters, betrayals and detours you are bound to meet on the way. And thank goodness you don't.

I happen to believe that all first-time entrepreneurs should be a little naive, because if they were truly aware of all the dangers facing them, they might forget the whole idea. You simply cannot anticipate every source of danger and every hidden trap between here and whatever goal you set for yourself when launching a business. The best thing you can do is underestimate the dangers they represent and remain convinced that you can handle them.

The stronger your vision, the more pain you can stand on the journey towards realizing it. For want of a better term, let's call it healthy ignorance. Some people may have another name for it. They may label it unqualified optimism or even blind idiocy. I'm not certain it's either. I believe that people who are convinced of their abilities and the validity of their vision accept the fact that they will encounter challenges and will minimize them when they occur. If you anticipate a problem and can convince yourself that it's not nearly as insurmountable as you feared when you finally bump into it, you're using positive thinking. Or perhaps some sort of psychological incentive.

But here we go getting hung up on labels again. So let's dispense with the labels. When it comes to positive thinking, I imagine an entrepreneur finding himself standing at the gates of Hell and thinking, "You know, it's not as hot down here as I expected . . ."

Six Rules for Driven Entrepreneurs

1. **Your idea needn't be totally original.** It should simply be distinctive and deliver unique benefits.
2. **Ideas that can be easily duplicated by others may have no value.** As soon as you achieve a notable degree of success, someone else with deeper pockets, more experience or an existing production/distribution system will, in Kevin O'Leary's favourite phrase, squash you like a cockroach.
3. **If it is not patentable, the opportunities for success are limited.**
4. **The odds are against you.** If this alone deters you, you are not sufficiently driven to succeed.

5. **Prepare yourself for the unexpected and unanticipated.** You cannot be fully aware of all the challenges you will face launching your company, bringing your product or service to market, and dealing with unimagined obstacles. And it's a good thing you aren't.

6. **Unless you can't wait to get started on building your business each day when you wake up, reconsider your goal.** People who manage to reach exceptional levels of success cannot imagine themselves doing anything else in life. Building their company is something less than work and something more than play.

9

Why You Should Work for Free— Sometimes

Sophie Tucker, a show-business legend from the last century, famously said, "I've been rich and I've been poor, and rich is better." I'm with Sophie.

Growing up with my grandparents in Croatia, I suppose they were poor, if living in a house with a dirt floor is a measure of poverty. They just didn't know it at the time, because almost everybody else in the village lived the same way they did. Somehow I always knew there was more, however. And I always knew I would find a way of living differently, enjoying the perks and pleasures that money could bring.

When I arrived with my parents in Toronto, the knowledge that success was attainable fed a passion to reach it. I didn't know how—I was never obsessed with a vision of myself as a successful banker or corporate lawyer or any specific profession.

I wanted to make lots of money on my own terms, not as a cog in a corporation.

I was willing to work hard to gain the chance of making money, but from an early age I knew that energy and ambition alone wouldn't be enough. The simple fact was that I honestly believed I would achieve success in business, and the belief grew into a passion with me. Of all the qualities needed to make it in business, none is more important than belief in yourself and passion to reach your goal.

At the beginning, my ambition was driven by money. Money to me was a means of keeping score; the more money I made, the better I was at playing the game. The interesting part of this tale is the fact that I opened the gates to achieving the wealth I have today by working for no income not once, but twice. I didn't know it at the time—how could I?—but by working without a salary I was sacrificing immediate income in return for knowledge and experience that would pay off years down the road.

The lesson here, I suppose, is to search for a career that ignites passion in you and, having identified it, do whatever is needed to equip yourself for a lifetime pursuing it. For some people, it's athletics. For others, it's music or medicine, writing or teaching, or some other career.

Mine happened to be computers. Not designing or selling them or writing programs for them or even using them. It was the dynamics of the industry itself that intrigued me, and persuaded me to make the sacrifices necessary to immerse myself in its dynamic growth. Including, as I noted, working for free.

At age twelve I was delivering newspapers to earn money when I read an article about the need for movie extras, which sounded much more profitable and a lot more fun than dragging a sack of newspapers from door to door every day. I urged my mother to enrol me with a talent agency. She invested money in acting lessons to give me a head start over all the other kids who wanted to be the next child star. I made a few television commercials, but the experience failed to be either profitable or glamorous. Too much time was spent waiting around for a talent agency or producer to call, and once I was on the set, more time was wasted while the director and crew got the lighting, sound and camera moves just right. I was bored. An acting career was not for me.

After university, I explored various paths leading to what I hoped would be the level of success I was after. Some were a matter of marking time and making enough money to survive until the opportunity arrived. I waited tables in a family restaurant and in an upscale bar frequented by high rollers. I sold high-end clothing at a major men's retail chain and worked the telephones for a collection agency, wringing money from people who had missed payments on their car or furniture. Later, I used my limited experience in TV commercials to grab a job as a go-fer on movie sets. When I moved into television, taking a job with the Global TV network, I qualified as a field producer to cover the 1984 Winter Olympics in Sarajevo on the basis of being the only guy in the crew who understood Croatian. Three weeks of preparation, followed by two weeks on snowy hills and in frigid arenas—all located not far from the village where I grew up—was fun, but the role of field producer failed to lure me into the TV business permanently.

In fact, none of these supposedly glamorous jobs held much interest for me. The movies paid well for a short time, but the work opportunities were spotty. Once a movie production was over, I hated the idea of sitting around waiting for another to arrive in town. Television wasn't much better. I kept waiting on tables at night and picking up whatever movie work I could find during the day.

One day, a major studio called me to work as an assistant to the director of a film production. The director was a macho guy with the swagger of John Wayne or Jack Nicholson but without their cool demeanour. He bragged about beating up movie star Gene Wilder when both were attending high school in Wisconsin, and he carried the same bullying attitude onto the movie set. Nothing anyone could do seemed to please him, everything that went wrong was somebody else's fault, and he had a habit of humiliating people by firing them in front of the rest of the crew, sometimes hiring them back later.

I knew about his abrasive personality. I was also becoming jaded with the movie business in general. The kind of money I wanted to make was available in movies, but that meant working in Hollywood, and I knew how many people my age were clamouring for work there. What chance did an immigrant kid in Canada have to make it big in Hollywood? Not much, so when the director got around to firing me halfway through the production, which I expected him to do, I said "Fine," walked off the set, and never went back. Good riddance to my movie career.

A couple of days later, I was talking to a friend named Steve, who had graduated with a degree in computer science a couple of years earlier. We both happened to be unemployed. He told me about a start-up company that sold boards that enable PCs to talk to mainframe computers. The guy who had started the company wanted somebody with computer experience and at least five years' sales experience.

I thought PC stood for "politically correct," and a mainframe sounded like something that held an automobile together. None of that mattered. Only two things registered with me: one was that the job involved sales, and I enjoyed selling; the other was that the job paid $30,000, which represented a substantial income at the time.

"Who is this guy?" I asked, "And how can I contact him?"

Locating a Route to Wealth

The next day, I arrived at a suburban Toronto office that claimed to be the new company's headquarters. I say "claimed" because as soon as I entered I saw only stacks of cardboard boxes and a small desk. Behind the desk sat Denis, the company founder, who had been a marketing executive with IBM before leaving to start his own firm.

I told Denis I was applying for the job Steve had told me about. I knew it related to computers, which seemed to offer more opportunity for future growth prospects than restaurants, men's clothing and movies.

"You seem like a nice kid," he said in his French-Canadian accent, "but you know nothing about computers and you don't have enough sales experience. Sorry."

"Okay, you're right," I said, and I pointed to all the boxes crowding the office, including the one I was sitting on. "But you need somebody to do stuff here, right?"

Denis agreed, and I said, "So hire me and I will do . . . stuff. I'll answer the phone, I'll do shipping—whatever needs to be done, I'll do it. Meanwhile, I'll learn all I need to know about computers from you and whoever else you hire. It'll take me maybe six months to pick up all the knowledge I need, and when that happens you can pay me the salary you offered Steve. How's that?"

I could tell by Denis's expression that he wasn't sold on the idea, so I added: "And I'll work for free."

I figured this would seal the deal, but Denis shook his head. "That's a nice thought," he said, "but if you work for free, I can't depend on you."

At that instant, something happened inside me. Somehow I realized that becoming a part of the computer revolution, as it was called at the time, represented my best opportunity to become as successful as I had dreamed. I couldn't leave that office without getting the job.

I looked directly at Denis and said, slowly and distinctly, "Oh, yes. You can depend on me."

To this day, I don't know if it was the tone of my voice, the expression on my face, or the audacity of my offer, but Denis replied, "Okay. I'll give you a chance."

I had located a route to wealth. I was uncertain of the destination or even the direction to follow, but I felt I was on the road to the kind of business success I had envisioned, and everything else in my life unfolded as though it were a movie script.

Denis didn't pay me for several months. I won't say I didn't care, but I wasn't upset, either. That was the deal and we both lived up to it.

I supported myself by waiting tables at Remys, an upscale bistro in Toronto's trendy Yorkville district. As soon as I finished my day working with Denis, I raced to Remys, where I worked until past one in the morning, earning enough money each week to cover my living expenses. Four and a half hours after crashing in my bed, I was back at the office with Denis, making coffee, checking customer reports, assessing inventory and generally absorbing everything I could. I loved every exhausting minute of it.

Each day at the office generated excitement in me. The computer industry was in the midst of perhaps its most dramatic phase, when personal computers were popping up in homes and offices almost faster than the manufacturers could produce them, and every new advance was like another magic trick to me. I could hardly wait to see what new rabbit was pulled out of the magician's hat.

I recognized, for the first time, that I had the ability to see how an industry will appear about eighteen months into the future, and the products and services that would be needed then. That's where big profits lie—not in the way things are today or were in the past, but in the way they will be a year or more from now.

If you entered the cellphone market five years ago and couldn't foresee the impact of the BlackBerry and text-messaging, you've been left behind. But if you can take your eyes off today's hot market and look a year and a half ahead in computers, electronics or any rapidly changing industry, you can get there ahead of the crowd. The best opportunities and biggest profits are not waiting outside your window as you read this book. They are eighteen months down the road, which is the perfect timeframe for you to assess the opportunity and gear up to meet it, starting today.

Either by birth or by experience, I possessed the ability to see far ahead where technology is concerned. It has helped make me successful, and I sincerely believe that if I could see two or three years ahead, I would be two or three times wealthier.

The Eight Biggest Myths About Running Your Own Business

1. **The product is so great it will sell itself.** Nothing gets sold until the person with the need and the ability to buy it learns about it.
2. **The best way to get rich quick is to start your own business.**
3. **If you make a profit in your first year, consider yourself lucky.**
4. **I'll be able to convince my bank to be my business partner.** Starting a new venture represents a risk. Banks don't take risks; they take the biggest spread possible in interest rates on loans that involve the lowest risk possible. They may be necessary, but they are not "perfect."
5. **I'll build my business with discounts to early customers and be able to catch up on pricing later on.** Once you offer a discount, it is very difficult to boost the price to the necessary level without losing money, customers—or both.
6. **I'll match or beat my competitors' prices and still make money.** Unless you know both your own and the competitors' margins, this is a losing proposition.
7. **My employees will be my friends.** You can be friendly with your employees, but you cannot be friends with them. Not if you want to operate a profitable and successful business.

8. **I'll have more free time when I'm my own boss.** Most business owners work harder, at longer hours, than they ever did working for someone else. The upside: they do it because they enjoy it.

10

The Power of Money and the Importance of Passion

It is impossible for any of us on the *Dragons' Den* panel to honestly state that the money we earn and the material benefits we enjoy don't matter to us. Of course they matter. Kevin O'Leary keeps repeating that he thinks of every dollar he invests as a soldier, and each morning all of his hundreds of millions of soldiers go out into the world to seize prisoners and bring them home before the sun goes down. I'm not quite as dedicated to the idea that each dollar I own must be profitable every day of the year, but I'm intent on seeing that they do as well as I expect them to do. Yet in my heart—and even in Kevin's, were he to admit it—money alone is not the ultimate reward. Beyond a certain level, the role of the money I earn is not immediately to buy me new things but to mark my progress on a scoreboard of sorts. If this sounds as though the entire process is something of a game, it's true. The vast majority of successful businesspeople make use of the same motivation that drives professional athletes and artists, and its primary symptom is obsession.

The Difference Between Ambition and Passion

Whenever I tell people about how I worked for nothing during the day and worked at a restaurant until late at night to earn money to survive, they usually tell me I have exceptional ambition.

I've never considered myself overly ambitious about work. Instead, I have found ways to be *passionate* about it.

Here's the difference: you're ambitious at your job when you're planning to reach some defined goal in your career or your income level; you're passionate about your work when you're focusing not on current income but on future possibilities. Being passionate means you're thinking of being the best at what you choose to do. You're always looking ahead to a future objective that may require some sacrifice today but will pay off with huge rewards later. This is a difficult concept for many people to deal with, because they are too easily satisfied by short-term rewards, so they abandon the idea of reaching long-term goals.

Someone I know very well once told me how impressed he was with my financial success. I was a model for him, and he planned to build a career using me as his inspiration. I wished him well and promised to help when and where I could.

The first job he accepted was a sales position. He was bright and ambitious, but lacked both the style and the wardrobe the job demanded. His manager suggested he buy himself a suit and dress in a more businesslike fashion than the image he had been projecting of himself, which was that of a college boy doing a summer job to earn tuition. My friend bought one suit, the only one he owned, and one shirt-and-tie combination to wear with it. After several days of seeing him in the same outfit, the sales manager advised him to purchase another suit.

My friend mentioned this to his father that evening. His dad's response was to ask who was paying for all these new clothes.

"I am," my friend replied.

This, his father preached, was not fair. Why should his son have to spend hard-earned money on clothes just to please some sales manager? If the employer wasn't prepared to cover the cost of the new wardrobe, my friend's father suggested maybe his son should look for another job.

And he did. He quit the sales job, which promised an opportunity to move into a management position with a substantial company, and went to work as an apprentice baker, which paid marginally more, without the need to buy new clothes.

Being a baker is a fine trade. Nothing wrong with it. But will it lead you to success, if money and an executive position are your goals? How much more will the world's best baker earn than the average journeyman butcher? Not much, I expect. My friend doesn't plan to open his own bakery. He's content to work for a large employer who, he is convinced, will assure him something close to a permanent job. I suspect that in ten years he'll be taking home a few more bucks each month, in today's dollars, than he's making today.

In my book, he made a short-sighted decision. Spending a few hundred dollars on a couple of presentable suits and building on his sales job might have opened the door to a salary ten times bigger than the one he left to become a baker.

My friend chose security over passion, and I can understand that approach to life. I just refuse to choose it for myself.

There are many sins in life, and each of us can categorize them as we see fit. In my book, unfulfilled potential is a sin. Simply put, it's throwing away all we could be if we cared enough to achieve it by harnessing enough passion.

Shooting Pucks, Hitting Tennis Balls and Becoming Rich

Beyond a certain point, the engine that keeps driving successful people forward isn't greed, it's a passion to become as successful at their work as they can possibly be.

We see this in professional sports over and over again. All those early mornings when a young Wayne Gretzky rose to practise his skating and shooting alone, while the rest of the world was still sleeping, weren't driven by a need to sign a multi-million-dollar contract. They were driven by passion for the game, and by a need to become the most successful hockey player of his generation. And who knows how many hours Venus and Serena Williams spent on the tennis court, volleying balls back and forth when, I suspect, they would have been happy dancing in a disco or just hanging out with their friends? You don't make it to the centre court at Wimbledon by spending time on a dance floor.

The money finally arrived for them, as it has for many other athletes. But the money was a by-product of the passion they felt a need to satisfy, and they satisfied it by working as hard as they could to travel as far as their talents would carry them.

Nothing of any consequence was ever achieved without enormous passion and total dedication, not to the goal of making money but to the objective of becoming nothing less than the best. Those who lack the necessary passion, or never search for it deeply enough in their souls, risk wasting their potential. And here's the gold at the end of the rainbow: when you become great at something you love, the money always follows. Even if you're a baker.

Many people ignore that idea and fix their eyes exclusively on making as much money as possible as soon as they can. The work itself, and their passion for it, is incidental to them. Since passion plays no role, they derive their incentive from some other source. They may depend on unions to negotiate their income levels and maximize their benefits, or immerse themselves in debt that needs to be paid off over several years. Along the way, they may lead contented lives and feel they have achieved all the success they need.

That's fine with me. But without intense passion for their work, whatever it may be, they will never become all they could be, and they will never reach their dreams. Or maybe they had none to begin with.

11

Embrace Chaos

A creative director I know used to keep a sign above his own untidy desk in his advertising agency. The sign read:

Chaos breeds life.
Order breeds habit.

Some people believed the sign was a rationale for his refusal to tidy up and organize his office every day. He insisted it reflected his philosophy that the best creative ideas came not from precise neatness but from a blend of often-unrelated subjects, and that the more access he had to these subjects in random order, the more ideas he could create. If he organized his materials according to chronology, the alphabet, the Dewey decimal system or some other rule, he would do so out of habit. And he hated habits of any kind.

Truly driven businesspeople don't fear chaos as much as they dislike habit. This may be difficult to grasp when the chaos spills over into their personal and family life, but it's true. To most people with families, it's comforting to have a routine, knowing what usually happens on Saturday mornings, what time dinner is served on weekday evenings, and where you expect to be tomorrow, next week, next month and next year.

Being driven to make a career in business, however, is very different, especially if your ambition is to achieve great heights of success. It can also be very difficult when your spouse and immediate family members do not share or understand your driven nature.

If one of your primary goals is to enjoy an ordered, predictable life, I suggest you abandon any plans to become a successful entrepreneur or launch a start-up company right now. In many ways you should be prepared not only to accept chaos in your life, but to embrace it. Welcome it. Thrive in it. And even profit from it.

Success out of Chaos

The U.S. Marine Corps, at one time, planned to use high-speed computers to help simulate battles and determine, as the battle progressed, the best strategy to follow on the field of conflict. What a concept! With such powerful reasoning, the generals believed they could plot every conceivable battlefield situation and know in advance the decisions that would lead to ultimate victory.

The plan failed miserably.

The problem wasn't with the computers or the people who programmed them. It wasn't with the generals who believed the idea was a good one. The snag, as anyone who has either been involved in combat or who studied famous historical battles in detail could have predicted, is the nature of the battlefield itself. Computers are logical and linear, working within established rules, which is why they still easily defeat the most gifted chess masters. In contrast, battles between large groups of combatants are illogical and chaotic.

If military strategy fails to demonstrate the importance of embracing chaos, just look at nature. Rainforests interact and evolve with their surroundings. Nothing is ordered or predictable in a rainforest, yet it is impossible to find any environment in the world that is so alive and responsive.

Okay, total chaos is a problem, not a goal. But it's pretty clear to me that things in business, and in life generally, are most productive when they occur in the narrow space between stability and disorder. Think of the offices of the most productive people you know. They're probably just a little messy. Or consider this: the happiest families I know have loud, active children and somewhat impulsive and indulgent parents. Would you expect a family whose members behaved as though they were members of a military regiment to be happy and content? Remember as well that the most robust economies grow with minimum rules and maximum opportunities for business to expand according to opportunity, not regulations.

You Either Get It or You Don't
(If You're Driven, You Get It)

Whenever I describe the chaos of creating and managing a start-up company, I can immediately separate the people who are driven to launch their own firm from those who would never consider the idea. People who are driven to succeed in business never question the fact that I thrive in the disorder and unpredictable environment of a new firm; those who lack passion for business cannot understand my tolerance for a little unstructured disorder.

Once you are enmeshed in a new start-up company, somewhere among your activities to make things work comes the suggestion that your operation is the most chaotic in the world. It almost certainly isn't (and how could you determine if it was?), but like most others in your position, you will probably consider it a badge of honour to believe that it is.

So why do it? Controlling chaos, or at least trying to, may be exciting and stimulating, but it is also frustrating, exasperating and rarely good for your blood pressure. Be forewarned, if necessary, that it leads to disrupted vacations, diminished social life, substantial stress, reduced immediate monetary returns and insomnia.

Beyond an apparent by-product of a driven personality, what is there about dealing with anarchy that continues to appeal to the driven personality?

The one-word answer: *opportunity.*

The two-word answer: *it's addictive.*

Anyone who prefers a calm, mature and stable work environment does so because he or she wants to leave the office at 5 p.m. each day. This is more important than seeking to benefit from unforeseeable opportunities and adrenalin-raising crises. They also, I suspect, value clearly defined roles and responsibilities, established priorities and the presence, when necessary, of experts.

If you are honestly driven, however, this kind of stuff is deadly boring. Grappling with crises and chaos, on the other hand, is honestly addictive. Knowing that the next telephone call could change both your company and your life forever generates its own emotional high, just as knowing that the person sitting on your left is your entire sales team and the person seated on your right is the sum total of your service and installation department.

This kind of thing either frightens or inspires you. If it frightens you, you will never truly understand what it means to be driven to succeed. If it inspires you, I suspect you are one of two types of people: either you are bored very easily and need constant motivation to remain engaged in your occupation, or you are not entirely certain what you want to do career-wise with your life, in which case I hope you are under thirty with few personal obligations.

How I Deal with the Stress of Running a Business

1. **I love what I do.** To me, stress is perception. I run a fast-growing technology-based company and appear on two network television shows. I'm also a husband and father with three active children, and I run marathons, among other activities. Some people assume my life is stressful, but they're wrong. I love what I do so much that I don't want the day to end, and I can't wait for tomorrow to begin.

2. **I need to be in the driver's seat.** Being in control does not create stress, it reduces it. I worked hard to get where I am today. I made it happen, and in that sense I imposed whatever stress I feel upon myself. This sense of control makes it easier to deal with pressure.

3. **I accept the inevitability of stress and deal with it.** My mother experienced stress throughout her life because, instead of dealing with stress, she tried to deny that it existed. As a result, she suffered terribly from migraines all through her working life. When she finally retired, she found herself stress-free—for about six months. Then the migraines returned, caused by housework, travel and worrying about me and my "stressful" life. She never learned how to cope with stress, and her inability to deal with it created problems throughout her life.

4. **I do everything I can to be fully informed.** I don't mind stress, but I hate surprises. If we fail to secure a deal I worked hard to win, I can handle the stress and disappointment. If we failed because of something that someone on our team knew about but failed to communicate to me, that's a different story. That's a form of stress that I cannot accept and rarely tolerate.

5. **I always remember that any problem that can be solved with money is not that serious.** I don't mean to dismiss the financial hardship experienced by many people. I experienced it myself as the son of poor immigrants. But as much as my parents and I struggled with economic demands, we balanced it by emphasizing other qualities, such as family and social contacts, and loving and supporting one another—lessons that, once learned, are never forgotten.

6. **I've found outlets for my stress.** During the economic downturn of 2008–09, I began to run marathons, and the demands of training and competing worked wonders on the

stress I was feeling. Trying to break through a wall of weariness and fatigue with another ten miles to run easily banishes any other worries that may have been crowding your mind. You don't have to run marathons to benefit from this; just push yourself to new limits. "If you are hard on yourself," I tell my employees, "life will be easy."

7. **I deal first with urgent concerns.** The biggest danger of stress is its ability to overwhelm you. If dealing with twenty important issues, I choose the most urgent and focus on solving it before moving to the second most urgent. This permits me to focus on a single task and, more important, gives me a sense of control over the situation.

8. **I don't panic.** Research has indicated that in situations ranging from plane crashes to bear attacks, those who panic have the least chance of survival. Panic is also contagious; if your employees sense panic on your part, they'll likely respond with the same emotion.

9. **When it's over, I analyze.** Whenever a perceived crisis erupts, I remind myself that I need to do two things: solve it, and eliminate the possibility of a repeat performance. When the dust clears and the blood pressure drops, I take time to analyze what happened, why it happened and how to prevent it happening again.

10. **I remind myself that the sun will still rise tomorrow.** Few business disasters threaten to black out either the sky or my life.

12

Seize Opportunity

In politics, calling someone an opportunist is neither a compliment nor a term of endearment. It suggests someone who will sacrifice principles in order to take advantage of an expedient situation. In business, an opportunist is someone not to be decried but admired for the ability to instantly recognize a situation, often fleeting, that can be exploited to establish or advance a business.

People driven to succeed tend to be opportunists, and refuse to apologize for it. Nor should they.

How many times have you had a flash of insight into something, a sudden realization that you have something to gain by acting quickly—not impulsively or irresponsibly, throwing all caution to the wind, but with the conviction that you know you are right, and whatever investment you make will be worth it?

It happens rarely. To some people, it never happens at all.

I suspect, however, that it happens most often to those of us driven to succeed. In that state of mind, perhaps we have a keener vision of the true value of whatever opportunity comes along, combined with the drive to take advantage of it.

Finding Opportunity at Thirty-five Thousand Feet

On board a flight to a trade show some years ago, I struck up a conversation with my seatmate, a man named Robert Metcalfe. Over the course of the flight, he revealed to me that he had developed a means of permitting different desktop computers to communicate with each other. He called it Ethernet.

At the time, the idea of personal computers networking was unheard of, and I took a few minutes to explore the implications. A company with a hundred or more personal computers located on desks, each performing tasks such as word processing, spreadsheet construction, graphic design and more, needed a dedicated printer for each computer. Good printers cost several thousand dollars each. With Ethernet connections, one printer could serve a dozen computers, generating huge savings.

Sharing files between computers represented another benefit. If someone on the tenth floor of a company with several computers had a file that someone on the third floor required, the file had to be copied onto a disk in the first computer and the disk carried to the second computer, where, it was hoped, the file could be opened, read and modified as needed. Networking eliminated the time, the energy and the errors.

Metcalfe planned to find representatives for his technology at the trade show, which attracted computer industry representatives from all over the world. I asked if he had anyone to represent the concept in Canada. When I learned he hadn't, I asked for the rights immediately while we were thirty-five thousand feet above Kansas. We agreed in principle and, upon landing in Las Vegas, I immediately exchanged my airline ticket for one on the flight back to Toronto. Within a few days I found partners to help me launch a new company based on providing Ethernet benefits to the exploding number of personal-computer users across Canada.

Pure luck seated me next to a visionary like Robert Metcalfe, and I'm not suggesting that I was the only one to immediately recognize the business potential of his concept. The important point was that I also realized the opportunity, and the need to act on it immediately.

Years later, with the expansion of the Internet into applications no one had imagined, I had another flash of insight. With such easy, instant access to data and resources, security will become a prime concern, and companies delivering superior Internet security would do exceptionally well. I immediately took steps to change the course of my business and become the industry leader in providing reliable security measures.

Not everyone shared my vision or the company's need to restructure to serve this market. As a result, half my staff left the firm. My concept appeared foolhardy to them, and while I regretted their departure I remained fixed on my goal for two reasons. First, I believed that even if I were mistaken, the company would survive. And second, I honestly believed I was correct. Of all the business decisions I have made in my life, none exceeds this one in impact and importance.

How effectively would you recognize a similar opportunity and benefit from it? Consider these guidelines:

- **All real opportunities are industry-related.** I can wake up every morning and name a business or sector in the computer security industry that is growing. No one, I'm convinced, can do the same thing in manufacturing in North America— which, as I write this, appears to be in serious decline. So when looking for opportunities, go where most are found. It's like fishing for dinner: you put your hook in a lake, not in a bathtub.
- **Use the resources you have today.** Are there new business opportunities in the design of passenger aircraft? Perhaps. Unless you are already in that industry in some capacity, assuming you can identify the opportunities isn't enough. You need access to people with names like Boeing and Bombardier to fully exploit them.
- **Understand the impact of the real world.** Many years ago, on the brink of the cellular telephone explosion, a business associate suggested that the cellphone industry represented a major investment opportunity. His proposal: we should start building and operating wireless telephone communication towers for use by the telephone carriers. Interesting, until I noted that the major competition to the operation would be Motorola. By every measure, going head to head with Motorola would be a losing proposition unless we had a unique advantage, and we hadn't. In technology, a company with no name recognition and limited capital investment would be a mouse to the Motorola elephant. I could see no way we could compete, let alone win. The opportunity was there, but it wasn't worth seizing.

We see these guidelines ignored over and over again on *Dragons'*
Den. Otherwise apparently intelligent people claim to possess an
opportunity that represents financial success and assume they
can profit from it. Unfortunately, too many of them ignore the
hard truths.

Ten Steps to Prepare for Opportunity

1. **Be aware.** The best business opportunities are never adver-
   tised and rarely appear on the evening news. Watch and listen
   carefully.
2. **Act quickly.** As bright and prepared as you may be, others are
   just as open to opportunities as you are. Take too long to react
   and they will be gone.
3. **Think it through.** Before you commit anything, understand
   what you must do and how you can profit. This conflicts with
   the previous point, but hey—if it were easy, everybody would
   be as wealthy as you want to be.
4. **Know your industry.** If you do not understand pharmaceuticals, manufacturing or wireless technology, do not invest in
   opportunities that arise in pharmaceuticals, manufacturing
   or wireless technology. Define the industries you know and
   look for opportunities there.
5. **Don't challenge giants.** No matter how promising the
   opportunity, if your business concept puts you in competition with established industry leaders, you are more likely to
   profit by joining them instead of competing against them.
6. **Appreciate the value of exclusivity.** The more easily your
   idea or concept can be copied, the less value it has. Patenting

and licensing are not perfect, but they have measurable worth.

7. **Gather your resources.** The less you have to do to prepare to take advantage of a business opportunity, the better your chance of success.

8. **Seek two kinds of capital.** You will probably require financing of some kind, whether it's from friends, from banks or from personal assets. That's one kind of capital. The other is business experience from partners who may take a minority interest in exchange for their expertise in marketing, manufacturing, distribution or other areas in which you are weak. This second kind of capital is equally valuable.

9. **Accept that opportunity does not equal success.** An opportunity is just that—a chance to achieve business success. Between the two are hard work, risk and a dozen other factors. If you're not prepared to take these steps, don't bother taking the first one.

10. **Realize that nobody knows everything.** No matter how much good advice you receive from various sources, including this book, some answers you'll have to find on your own.

13

Learn from Failure, Profit from Change

Experience may be a good teacher, but its lessons are often painful. The best way to dull the pain of a business failure is to isolate the cause, identify the lesson learned, and change your policies, strategies or processes to deliver future success.

You learn from your victories as well as your failures, but the lessons are never as powerful or as valuable. Businesspeople can take lessons from successful athletes such as Michael Jordan, perhaps the greatest professional basketball player of all time.

Jordan was great, but he wasn't perfect. At the end of his career he could recall almost every free throw he missed and every occasion when he was handed the ball near the end of the game, given an opportunity to score the winning basket . . . and missed. "I failed over and over and over in my career," he said. "That's why I succeeded." Not just because he kept going, but because he learned something from every failure.

I Confess: Not Every Business Decision I Have Made Has Been Successful

My experience over twenty years of launching and operating businesses taught me the importance of sharpening and maintaining focus on what I really wanted. Did I succeed with every decision I made over that time? Hardly. Nobody does, nor should anybody expect to.

It's important, however, to recognize that not succeeding at a goal or not making the correct decision doesn't necessarily qualify as failure. Remarkably few people recognize this fact. Why? **Because they're too frightened of imminent failure to aim for future success.**

If you're sufficiently driven to succeed, you won't have that problem. Most successful people never dwell on failure, because their belief in themselves is so powerful, and they are so confident they will succeed in the end, that they are almost delusional.

Around the time I grew determined to launch my own firm, I had a long discussion with one of my best friends, who was working for a large appliance company. When I asked how things were going in his career, he shrugged, smiled and told me the company had offered him the position of regional director, three levels above his current job.

"That's great," I responded. "When do you start?"

"I don't," my friend replied. "I turned it down."

I couldn't believe it. How could he reject such a major promotion? Aside from the salary increase he could expect, think of the experience it would provide, the things he would learn, the people he could connect with. Why would he not take advantage of such an opportunity?

"Because," he replied, "I don't want to take on a job I may not be ready for. If I fail at it, I may never get the opportunity again. So I'd rather learn as much as I can and, when I'm ready for the job, that's when I'll go."

I thought he was crazy and told him so, friend to friend. "You say if you fail, you may never get the opportunity again," I said. "But when you think you're ready, how do you know the opportunity will be there?"

What he had to do, I said, was take the job and forget about the chance of failing. The way I saw it, he couldn't lose. If he succeeded at the new job, he would be fast-tracked to a terrific career with the company, assuming that's what he wanted. And if he failed, he would learn so much from the experience that he could go after another job with new confidence.

He didn't buy it. Risk, he believed, was something you minimized. Risk, I believe, is something you exploit. It's all a matter of how much risk you are willing to accept, and how badly you want to exploit it.

My friend also, I suspect, wanted to avoid a massive change in his life and work. A small change—say, moving up one level in the corporate hierarchy—would be acceptable. A major change, which climbing up three levels would certainly represent, would be challenging. But a total change, including a new position with an entirely new company and industry, could be traumatic.

I can understand the fear of change some people feel. I just refuse to accept it.

I recalled my friend and his attitude recently when speaking at my daughter's school about the keys to success—what they were, where they are found and how to use them. "I believe," I said, "that the world will be won not by the weak, not by the strong or the mighty or the poor or the righteous, but by those who can adapt to change."

The children, I suspect, grasped the point of my message faster and more deeply than my friend did all those years ago.

Experience Is a Good Teacher, but It's a Cruel One as Well

Let's accept that you'll experience your share of failures through your business career, an expectation that's more likely among people starting new companies than those managing established operations. Let's also accept that minimizing the number of failures you encounter is a good move. Why pay for lessons you don't need?

The most catastrophic failure, of course, is the failure of your business. You could gain a thousand lessons from that, but they still won't be worth the price.

After twenty years of manoeuvring my way through various business minefields, watching other entrepreneurs score successes and survive failures, and experiencing my own stumbles from time to time, I've totalled twelve hurdles that businesses must overcome to survive. Given sufficient time and energy, you may be able to handle two or three of these challenges, learn your lesson, make the necessary corrections and sail past potential disaster to success. More than these, however, and you may well be doomed.

So here they are. Think of them as lessons from experience without having to suffer the experience yourself. The list is by no means comprehensive—there are many, many reasons why businesses fail—but it provides an overview.

- **Undercapitalization.** Most companies start on a shoestring, with insufficient capital to grow by taking advantage of opportunities. The fact that many entrepreneurs overestimate the degree of success they expect to achieve makes the problem even worse.
- **Lack of industry experience.** Every year that your competitors have been around longer than you is another year in which they've learned how to do things correctly and avoid doing things wrong. You may bring fresh thinking, which is good, but do not underestimate the impact of experience.
- **Lack of management experience.** It's easy to identify the wrong way to manage a company. It's far more difficult to identify the correct way to manage one and to implement all the ideas you know (or hope) are needed.
- **Poor record-keeping and financial control.** You may believe your company is doing well, but until you can gather the necessary data and know how to evaluate it, you are driving blind through a blizzard.
- **Ineffective planning.** Some businesspeople take pride in flying by the seat of their pants, making adjustments as they go. It may be exhilarating, but it's also limiting. The most successful companies achieve greatness by developing plans and strategies, communicating them to key members of their organization and aiming for performance targets.
- **Inadequate education.** A college or university degree doesn't guarantee success, but it tends to reduce the incidence of failure.
- **Poor staffing.** Successful companies have more than brilliant founders and CEOs guiding them. They boast talent

from top to bottom. This becomes a constantly growing strength, because good talent attracts other good talent. The better you can make every employee in terms of education, abilities, qualifications and dedication, the better you can build your company.

- **Unwise product/service timing.** Timing really is everything, both in business and in comedy. History is strewn with companies whose concepts and execution were great but whose products or services were either too late or too early for customers to appreciate.

- **Unwise economic timing.** It seems obvious, but it's worth noting: you have a better chance of succeeding in business when the economy is growing than when it's shrinking. The opposite can also be true—my last three businesses were all started in the midst of bad economies, when people are often more open to new products or services that can potentially save them money. But friendships and loyalty tend to go out the window in a bad economy.

- **Unwise personal timing.** Youth brings energy, but age brings wisdom. Most companies succeed when the founder is at the right age to bring equal quantities of both to the table. But remember: energy isn't exclusively reserved for the young, nor is wisdom guaranteed to the old. The "right age" can be sixty-five for some of us, as we'll see later in the book.

- **Lack of marketing skills.** As much as you may know about design, management, scheduling, production and a dozen other skills, if you don't understand how to market yourself, your company and your product, your chance of success is severely constrained.

- **Lack of partners.** If you can locate a compatible partner who is strong in skills where you are weak, and vice versa, you enhance your possibilities.

14

Be Your Own Boss

Most people in business harbour a dream of working for themselves someday. The freedom to make decisions, to fulfill a vision and maximize their earning potential, overrides concerns about security and risk. The day you begin to be your own boss is the first day on your journey to acquiring wealth.

(Incidentally, there are many different ways to start working for yourself. One is to have options or equity in the business you work for, making you something of a "partner" in that company. I think this is an important point to consider when re-evaluating your career. A company that offers equity may not guarantee you the brass ring, but some chance is better than no chance at all.)

Entrepreneurs love to trade stories of people who identified a business opportunity and developed it into not only a substantial success but an entirely new industry. One of the most accomplished of these people, although not necessarily the best known, was Warren Avis.

Avis had been a bomber pilot in the air force during the Second World War. He observed that whenever he flew somewhere— whether aboard a military flight or a civilian aircraft—unless he was landing at his home base where he had left his car, he would have to use either military or public transportation to leave the airport. Taking a bus, taxi or subway from an airport wasn't Warren's style. Nor, he suspected when he was discharged from the service, would it suit the millions of people who would be flying on commercial aircraft in the post-war years. They would prefer the freedom and convenience of renting a car.

Car rental agencies had been around about as long as commercial airlines, but they were located in the downtown cores of cities. Warren Avis recognized the opportunity to combine the two, enabling travellers to walk off an airplane and drive away in a rented car. Like all great ideas, it seems obvious to us now, but it was considered revolutionary when first introduced.

Avis's name remains on one of the largest car-rental firms in the world, although he sold the company in 1954, pocketing $8 million for his one very good idea. More than fifty-five years ago that was a substantial fortune, and Warren managed to add significantly to it through careful investments in electronics companies, real estate and other ventures.

I met Warren early in my career, and we hit it off. In fact, I worked with him for a short time. Later, he provided badly needed venture capital for one of my companies. He also offered some advice that's worth passing along.

"Most people spend their entire life working for somebody else," Avis said. "They think they're working for themselves and their family. They're not. They're working for the banks, the leasing companies, almost everybody but themselves. The true path to wealth is to stop working for others first. I mean, stop leasing cars and other items, and stop paying mortgages."

When you have a mortgage on your home or a lease on your car, Warren explained, you're working for people who are making an income from the money you're paying them. "The goal," he went on, "is to reach a point in your life where every dollar you make is your dollar. Not the bank's or the leasing company's. It's your dollar, and you get to keep all of the dollars you earn, subject to the tax man."

It's an interesting perspective, and one that may be impractical for most people, especially during their early adult years. Perhaps a realistic extension of Warren's point would be to try and lease or rent those items you can write off, and buy the things you can't. But being able to pay cash whenever possible does remain a goal worth aiming for.

15

Your Customers Always Come First

Every experience in life brings a lesson with it. Most lessons are either basic or incidental; a few are startling and traumatic. The true value of many lessons is not recognized until much later, when you are engaged in something totally unrelated to the original activity. The important thing about lessons is not to ignore them or assume they have no application, but to grasp their significance and use them where appropriate.

Some of the lessons I learned and apply to my businesses did not grow directly from the industries my companies served, but from jobs I held when I was more concerned about paying my rent than about building capital. One of these early careers included working as a waiter for two very different kinds of restaurants, where I learned how to deal with many problems I encounter today.

Is there really a connection between a chicken dinner and running a successful business? Yes, there is. The connection is the customer, and you can maximize your earnings and retain the customer's business using principles that apply equally to waiting tables and making executive decisions.

Start with a basic tenet: Know how and where the money is made, and focus your efforts accordingly.

To waiters—and people in the hospitality industry generally—the tips they earn represent the real reason to be in the business. If you can't earn tips, either directly or by sharing in the pool, find another line of work. Here's another link with business: by and large, the better you perform at your job, the more money you'll put in your pocket at the end of the day, thanks to tips from satisfied customers—not always, but often enough to reward you for the extra effort.

Choosing to work as a waiter at an exclusive club in Toronto's trendy Yorkville area and at a suburban St-Hubert chicken franchise were practical decisions on my part. Headquartered in Montreal, St-Hubert operated several franchises in the Toronto area during the 1970s and 1980s. They have since withdrawn from that region and are now almost exclusively a Quebec-based operation once again.

Out of university and still pondering what to do with my life, I had no interest in managing a restaurant, and even less in being a waiter for one day longer than necessary. Yet over the course of twenty-five years since then, I have often reflected on things I learned about people, about business and about myself while waiting on tables. I won't say the experiences were totally responsible for my business success, but I draw upon them from time to time when making a business decision or assessing a situation.

The first thing you learn as a waiter is not the menu or the chef's name; it's the importance of earning tips. Tips are the monetary lifeblood for waiters and bartenders, and when people learn that I worked in those two restaurants, one for Yorkville high rollers and the other for suburban middle-class families, they assume I earned more in tips in Yorkville. After all, the price of one of Remys' fancier cocktails could buy you an entire St-Hubert dinner. The tips at the club just have to be bigger, right?

Wrong. It wasn't always the case, but at the end of the night I tended to pocket more in tips at St-Hubert.

At St-Hubert, I might serve more than forty groups, mostly families, in one shift. At the Yorkville establishment, I'd serve perhaps four or five, some of them taking up my entire evening. True, the cheques at the club could reach $1,000 or more, but all my eggs were in only a couple of baskets. With the increased potential reward came greater risk; the margin for error was therefore narrower.

If I did a great job with the customer in Yorkville, I could expect (but not necessarily count on) a fat tip. But if something went wrong, even if it wasn't my fault—such as a steak being overcooked or the kitchen running out of a popular menu item—the tip could be next to nothing (and sometimes nothing at all). Even when everything went perfectly, there was no guarantee of a tip.

Similar things could occur at St-Hubert, but the impact of one bad meal or customer experience was much less, because each of my tables might turn over a dozen times in the course of a shift.

My restaurant experience provides a basic lesson about the importance of volume and diversification in business. Suppose your business has forty clients of roughly equal size generating $10 million annually—an average of $250,000 per client. Now imagine generating the same sales volume from just five clients, each of them delivering $2 million in business. No matter how attentive you are with your service, you would expect the $2-million customers to be more demanding; they would certainly justify more service in response to the size of their accounts. If you disappoint a client with poor product or bad service, the result will be more damaging to your volume with the big clients than with the little guys.

For a period of time, my company depended upon a single client for 25 per cent of our business, a situation that kept me awake at night. I was concerned that if we lost this one client, the company would be devastated. It was an echo of my experience as a waiter. I was more comfortable (and earned more tips) waiting on twenty tables each night at St-Hubert than four at the upscale restaurant, where one error could cost me almost half the night's income in tips.

A Difference Between Dining and Entertaining

Another lesson from the restaurants had as much to do with human nature as with business management.

St-Hubert was a family-oriented place, and, while families all have their own individual dynamics, members rarely do things to impress each other at a restaurant meal. They were therefore forgiving when something wasn't quite the way they wanted it.

At a higher-end restaurant, however, the situation changes dramatically. People aren't there just for a good meal at a good price. If that's all they wanted, they'd be at a family restaurant. The patrons at the high-end club were there for an experience, and much of that experience included entertaining and impressing others, meaning their own guests and diners seated at the next table. One of the ways many of them sought to impress their dates, guests or other diners was to ride roughshod over the waiter—meaning me—if something disappointed them. I had more to gain from the upscale diners if things were fine, and much more to lose when even the smallest thing went wrong.

Good waiters learn to read people in these situations, and boost their opportunities for a bigger sale and a correspondingly larger tip. If I encountered a man who appeared to know little about wine and was obviously trying to impress his girlfriend or business client, I would thank him for coming in and suggest a wine with the meal. My suggestion would be sensible—"Since you are both having a seafood entrée, may I suggest perhaps a nice Chardonnay with your dinner?"—but I would subtly steer him towards the higher end of the pricing as well ("For a special occasion such as this one, I think you would really appreciate the quality of the Bordeaux.").

This wasn't manipulation. It was upselling, a means of improving the customer experience while coincidentally improving the restaurant's—and my own—income potential.

Even more valuable than the extra tips I earned from those days and nights on a restaurant floor was the experience of learning how to read people and respond to their expectations. If a group of friends came in for a fun night on the town, I'd do my best to add to the merriment, making jokes and generally supporting the mood. I would alter my mood and my menu suggestions for a couple obviously out for a romantic evening, or for a couple of business heavyweights ready to discuss or finalize a business deal in privacy or impress a prospective new client.

This ability to read people is old hat to experienced waiters. It's also part of the basic skill set for good salespeople, and in my future business dealings I applied this knowledge in more ways than I can count. Similarly, I came to understand that customers pay for happy and not for sad. One of the keys to getting a good tip was to remember that no one cared if I was having a bad day. It wasn't their problem. To sum it up, good waiters and good salespeople are a little like chameleons, who can change their colours—or in this case their mannerisms and behaviour—to adapt to different situations. That's an important element of both personal and business dealings.

By the way, here's another skill picked up from all those evenings at St-Hubert: I can still carry eight plates piled with food to the table in one trip.

Rules of Waitering That Apply to Business

- **You don't get to choose your customers.** All restaurants seat diners to fill up the general area, not according to the skills of the waiter. Learn to accept that some people will be more satisfied than others, some will tip better than others, and all will expect you to meet their needs. Selling to people who share your interests is easy. Selling to people with whom you have nothing in common isn't, but it's necessary.

- **The customer isn't always right.** It's more important to make the customer feel good. If a diner was in a hurry for his meal and it took twice as long to arrive as it should have, the waiter can do something to correct the situation. Dozens of things can happen to upset customers, and they all did while I was a waiter, but rarely did a diner leave the restaurant feeling anything but positive. A free dessert or drink, and a sincere show of concern on my part, always overcame complaints.

- **The most important person to improve customer service is the person serving the customer.** Most customers with complaints don't want to make a fuss over it, such as by dealing with the restaurant manager. They want to focus on someone who understands their concern and can solve it on the spot. The most impressive example of this philosophy is the policy of the Four Seasons luxury hotel chain, which empowers any doorman at its properties to comp a guest's stay if the guest's experience has been sufficiently below the hotel's standards.

- **The buck stops at the customer service person.** Good waiters accept responsibility when things go wrong, even when it is clearly not their fault. Success as a waiter and as a business operator consists of reaching an ideal goal in an imperfect world. If the chef or production manager makes an error, whoever deals with the customer must accept responsibility for both the error and the solution.

- **Rudeness loses.** No bill of rights exists that says customers must be polite. Some are rude. But being rude back to a customer solves nothing. Managing to be pleasant and civil in the presence of rudeness, on the other hand, can provide surprising rewards.

- **Never appear overwhelmed, even when you are.** Diners and customers alike value coolness under pressure. If you must have a breakdown, throw a tantrum or just stop to take a deep breath, always do it in the kitchen (or alone in the boardroom), never in the dining area.

16

Honesty Is Still the Best Policy

I like to think the basic goodness in people—a sense of fair play, empathy for the concerns of others, and so on—helps them become better businesspeople by linking the demands of business with the qualities of compassion.

But in business, and in life generally, our trust is often misplaced. Even though experience teaches us to be wary of some promises we made in certain circumstances, we are often surprised and disappointed at unexpected betrayals. Business and life are both very complex and incredibly dynamic. Elements are in a constant state of flux. If a purchasing agent tells me I am getting the order and then I don't, it's not that he intentionally lied; it's more likely that variables changed that he was not even aware of. "Trust everyone but verify everything" is my motto.

That said, we can't go through life, and we can't grow and maintain a successful business, by wrapping ourselves in a thick cloak of suspicion. Trust is the basis of all rewarding relationships, and it's a necessity in most aspects of business. All we can do is prepare for betrayal and deal with it whenever it occurs. And if you stay in business long enough, and deal with a large enough sector of society, you'll encounter betrayals.

When this happens, do not assume that civil law will settle the question of who is right and who is wrong. The law is better at determining who has the most effective legal counsel or the most patience.

Some situations, of course, do not involve the law at all, but they do involve ethics. Or sometimes it's just the result of stretching the truth close to the breaking point.

Pitchers on the *Dragons' Den,* who come seeking investment money, are expected to be open and honest when answering questions about the status of their business. It's important for us to know how many sales they have recorded, how exclusive their product or service is, and other information that will affect our decision to provide the financial help they need.

We expect them to be totally honest, and most are. Before we hand over a cheque, however, we perform due diligence to confirm their claims and perhaps uncover a few negative facts they chose not to pass along. Most people are up front with us, but a few have been caught exaggerating their situations. And from time to time some unacknowledged complexities come up.

All five Dragons, for example, were enthusiastic about a powered unicycle brought to us by a very bright student named Ben Gulak. He had developed an electric-powered unicycle called—logically—the Uno. Between Ben's obvious brilliance and the product's irresistible appeal, we offered him $1.25 million for just

20 per cent of his business, an unprecedented amount of money for a minority position.

Due diligence confirmed Ben's involvement in the machine and its capabilities, but it also uncovered the fact that the Uno used components protected under a few dozen different patents held by others. On its own, this did not negate Ben's achievement. Complex technologies such as the one he had developed frequently employ a number of patented devices and systems. I'm convinced he had no idea of the number of patents involved, and there was never any hint that he intended to deceive us about it. The problem was one of delaying our return, because the Uno could not safely be launched and marketed until all the patent questions were answered, a process that could take decades, not to mention cost millions of dollars. With that awareness, four of us bailed out, leaving Brett Wilson the sole investor.

When Business Changes from Hardball
to Total Dishonesty

The pitchers on *Dragons' Den* want to present themselves and their businesses in the very best light, and that's understandable. It's also reasonable that competitors and negotiators will play hardball with each other in an effort to win the best deal possible.

Some experiences in business, however, exceed the limits of both understanding and reason. They are deceitful and corrupt, and you should be prepared to encounter them from time to time.

Sometimes an event happens in our lives that is so unexpected, so unfair and so bewildering that we don't know how to react. We're not angry, we're not crushed, we're not anything except so shocked that we can't even speak. I've seen this happen on *Dragons' Den*. People appear on the show after sinking years of labour and thousands of dollars into an idea that their friends and family have assured them is so brilliant, so revolutionary, so exceptional that it can't possibly fail. They step before the other panellists and me, begin their pitch, roar ahead brimming with confidence, and before they can finish their presentation our reaction is, "It's a dumb idea."

They cannot believe they are hearing those words. Yet, up and down the panel we all repeat variations on the same phrase— "Forget about it" and "What made you think this would work?" and "Nobody is ever going to buy this thing." The expression on their face suggests their soul has been sucked out of them. They don't know what to do or how to react. They don't cry, they don't plead, they don't shout in anger. They just wear a look of not understanding or believing what is happening to them.

Test Everything You Are Told

Everyone tells lies for every reason imaginable. We all know this in our hearts because we do it ourselves, and we are able to rationalize the telling of lies with various excuses. We didn't want to hurt someone's feelings. We made somebody feel good with a false compliment. We will find a way to make up for it someday in the future. We all know the reasons.

As a businessperson with a new—and likely struggling— company, however, you are more susceptible than others to damage caused by lies. The business world is crowded with stories of owners whose companies suffered when they expanded their capacity or loaded up on raw materials based on a lie told by a prospective customer. Similar stories exist about entrepreneurs believing investors' assurances that money is on the way to finance a new venture. Hundreds of variations on these tales are traded every day, most with depressing consequences.

In many cases, the person delivering the lie didn't mean to create a problem. They may have intended nothing more than encouragement or support. It doesn't matter. The damage can be just as devastating.

My advice: test everything you are told. If someone tells you they are preparing to invest in your business, thank them. Then ask them to provide the date when you can expect to receive the money, and avoid committing an expenditure based on the investment until the cheque has arrived and has cleared. If a client promises an order, ask whether it is in procurement yet and whether you are permitted to contact the purchasing agent to finalize details. Do this in a businesslike, not a suspicious, manner.

Six Steps to a Successful Business Partnership

Start-up companies with business partners have a better chance of succeeding than those with a solo entrepreneur or operator. Partners can bring a wider base of expertise and experience, greater financial resources, and a sharing of responsibilities—all critical components to a new venture. They can also complicate decision-making and, if the new partner is an unknown quantity, bring disaster in various forms. Whether your potential partner is on board from the beginning or seeks to join your operation when it is up and running, treat the opportunity with care. An unscrupulous partner can do more than damage or ruin your company; he or she can severely tarnish your reputation.

Before committing to any business partnership, follow these six steps.

1. **Speak a little and listen a lot.** Schedule a series of meetings before making a decision to partner with someone you do not know very well. Listen for verbal red flags—claims by your potential partner that may not ring true, such as tall tales of past achievements, unrealistic expectations of the partnership's future, and inconsistencies.

2. **Exchange resumés.** You need to know your partner's experience and capabilities, and he or she should have yours as well. An open approach to who you are and what you are bringing to the partnership builds trust and reasonable expectations.

3. **Check references.** Don't feel hesitant about confirming a future partner's claims. You would (or should) do the same thing with a new employee.

4. **Look into their background.** You don't need private detectives; an Internet search may reveal everything you need. You're interested in things others wouldn't reveal, including civil actions, criminal charges and critical personal data that had not been provided to you.

5. **Employ two lawyers—yours and theirs.** Legal agreements won't eliminate every concern, but your own lawyer may identify areas to be addressed in your interest, just as your partner's will.

6. **Never assign or accept exclusive tasks.** Every partner should be involved in both critical decision-making and executive activities in the company. Do not agree, for example, that a partner is exclusively responsible for financial matters without your involvement. You do not need to share in carrying out these important duties. You do need, however, to share in understanding and evaluating them.

17

The World—and Your Business—Doesn't Need Another You

My appearances on *Dragons' Den* have created a new challenge when I recruit and hire people for my business. Like it or not, the investors on *Dragons' Den* have become models for many prospective employees. We may be flattered to have people tell us "I want to be just like you," but it doesn't lead to great confidence in choosing them to be part of other teams.

Many of these people sincerely believe that they can absorb some of my or Kevin O'Leary's or Daymond John's success just by being close to us through their position in the company. The truth is, I don't want people in my company who want to be me. I want people who want to be themselves, who want to achieve something on their own terms and are willing to learn from me.

Some people who profess that they want to be Robert Herjavec see an association with me as a shortcut to the level of success I have achieved. I welcome the idea that anyone, including my own employees, wants to match the same degree of success I have managed to reach. I don't want them to see me as a shortcut, however, because **there are no shortcuts.** People who believe in a quick path to success are not the ones committed to performing the necessary hard work to get there. I prefer that they see me, and their career with my company, as part of the journey they are taking towards their goal, whatever it may be.

It's not easy to manage employees effectively. If it were, every employer would have a full staff of people working at top efficiency every hour of every working day. Sometimes I hear other entrepreneurs grumbling about managing their staff and suggesting they would prefer to build their company as a one-person operation. I can understand the frustration, but the idea is hardly practical. You cannot scale your company on your own.

Become Your Competition

I may try to dissuade employees from wanting to be me in some fashion, but I'm all for copying whatever the competition comes up with that is successful.

It's not my intention to rip off someone else's program or product—something I would never do nor allow my employees to do. If I discover that my competitor is scoring points at my expense, however, by using an approach that hadn't occurred to me, I won't just determine what it is, I'll figure out a way for my firm to use it, abandon my old idea by the side of the road and score points of my own.

Some aspects of technology aside, there is no such thing as a totally original idea. Besides, why create mediocrity if you can copy genius?

18

Be the Hot Dog Supplier,
Not the Hot Dog Stand

In business, you are doing one of two things. You are either growing or dying. Or, if you're a shark, you keep moving or you suffocate.

It sounds harsh, but it's true. The day Walmart or Microsoft or General Electric ceases to expand is the day the company begins to die. The symptoms may not be immediately apparent; in fact, they may take years to become obvious. But unless the situation is turned around, the result is inevitable. Growth is essential to survival in business, and every businessperson aiming for ultimate success had better grasp that idea and act accordingly.

This message was delivered with great effectiveness many years ago, when I was trying to establish myself in business, by Ross Marsden, chairman of Wang Canada at the time. Ross, whose business skills I admire very much and who remains a personal friend, was visiting me in my office. During our conversation, I mentioned my ambition to become a major player in the computer industry. "You're great at what you do," Ross said, "but you are never going to run a large company."

This came as something of a shock to me. I trusted Ross's instincts. How could I deal with his opinion that I would never realize my dream? I asked him why he made such a statement.

He looked out the window and down to the street in front of the building, where a man with a wheeled cart stood turning sausages and frankfurters on a portable barbecue. "See that hot dog vendor down there?" he asked.

I told him yes, I could see the vendor.

"He makes good hot dogs," Ross said. "So do you, in your own way. In fact, you're the best hot dog vendor in the city. You do a fantastic job. You know your hot dogs, you know how to cook them and how to sell them. But no matter how well you do your job, and how much better you are at it than others, you will never be more than a guy selling hot dogs on one corner of the city."

He turned back to face me. "So you have to ask yourself," he said, "do you want to be just another hot dog vendor on another corner selling hot dogs to people passing by? Or do you want to be the guy who sells hot dogs and buns and mustard to every hot dog vendor on every corner?"

The difference, he explained, was a matter of scale, and that's what I needed to learn: how to scale the company to a dominant size and, as I understand now, how to locate and motivate people to help me do it. Scaling the company larger demanded growth and, once started, growth must be continuous and effective.

I have no idea how contented that hot dog vendor was with his business. He may have been quite satisfied. But he would never achieve the same degree of success that true entrepreneurs crave. Not as long as he kept selling hot dogs to the same clientele from the same corner of the same city day after day.

19

Train for a Marathon, Prepare for a Sprint

The passion to succeed in business may be labelled in a number of ways—stubbornness, obsession, bullheadedness, persistence or determination. It makes no difference what you call it, it remains as essential as oxygen and water to anyone facing the inevitable challenges of launching and building an enterprise.

While **not everyone is born to be an entrepreneur**, or even an independent businessperson, they can become one under various circumstances. In contrast, the passion to succeed cannot be learned or acquired. It is either within you or it isn't. Whether this is a genetic disposition isn't for me to say. Some of the most passionate people in business and in the arts have been the sons and daughters of parents who appeared uninterested in pursuing excellence and achievement.

I believe, however, that passion plays a role in the degree of happiness we feel. To me, life is perfect when your passion is married to whatever you choose to pursue, and it is miserable when the things you must do to survive are at odds with your passion.

Managers vs. Entrepreneurs

I created my company out of the immediate necessity to earn an income, but I was not going against my own nature and instincts. Looking back, I believe my decision might have been inevitable because I was totally focused on achieving success on my own terms.

You can achieve success by working in an existing organization. It's done every day. This involves shaping your goals and ideals to somebody else's definition. That's fine if your goal is to be a successful manager. But successful managers are not driven entrepreneurs by any means. The two are almost different species. They think differently, they act differently, they measure success differently.

Effective managers are able to concentrate on one element and stay with it until they find a solution. Assign a good manager to reduce overhead, improve response to customer enquiries or optimize staff time on a given function, and he or she will find a way to do it by focusing on that single topic.

The entrepreneurial mind doesn't think that way. Tell a full-fledged entrepreneur to cut overhead, and he or she may begin looking at rents and wondering, perhaps, if there is a better way to divide floor space for maximum usage by a determined number of people. If the entrepreneur is a software engineer, he or she might see a software development opportunity there—maybe even an application for home design. Soon they're asking themselves, what if architects could insert a formula into a floor plan that would locate and size washrooms and kitchens to create more space for living rooms?

After an hour or so, the entrepreneur may be thinking of names for the software and speculating on who could be found to write it in exchange for partnership in a company that could become the Microsoft of the home-building industry.

Meanwhile, the good manager would be drafting expense account guidelines and finding a dozen other ways to save a few dollars here and there, by focusing exclusively on each decision's impact on the company's bottom line.

Entrepreneurs don't spend as much time examining their company's bottom lines as managers do because, when you are making your vision and dreams come true, you're not as focused on managing your company as on creating it.

Here's another idea: people with the outlook of an entrepreneur are not as numerous as those who think only in terms of managing. That explains why every year sees publishers put out ten times as many books about how to run a business than how to launch one. You can learn to run a business from a book; but if you lack the drive and passion of an entrepreneur, I'm not sure any book can inspire you to become one. (Not even this one!)

I often think of traditional managers as marathon runners, people who pace themselves over the long haul, unconcerned about who may be passing them at any given moment because their strategy is fixed. Many decisions wait to be made in running a marathon, and they are made according to a plan.

People who launch their own businesses from scratch, however, aren't marathon runners. They're sprinters. They can see the target just down the track. Pace themselves? Hardly. Their goal is to get from point A to point B ahead of everybody else, and the only way to achieve this is by running flat out, being in front when the starting gun fires *and* first across the line.

Many new businesses need the patience and endurance of a marathon runner, especially for new businesses that are still feeling their way. It's easy to become caught up in all the fervour of a first large order or the first big client contract, events that are usually followed by a lot of slapping of backs and popping of corks. You've completed the 100-metre dash. But now it's time to pace yourself for the distance. This includes checking every detail of the agreement, ensuring that every promise you made is kept and that all the euphoria of doing the deal doesn't overwhelm the reason you went into business: to build a success.

In essence, you have to take off your entrepreneur hat and put on a manager's hat. Or, if you prefer, kick off your sprinting shoes and lace up your long-distance shoes.

While managers are reviewing the multiple steps necessary to implement an idea, entrepreneurs have already made the decision and moved on to the next challenge. Entrepreneurs don't worry about making great decisions as much as they do about making fast decisions.

Sometimes It's a Little Like a Midway Game

What's the single most important thing to deal with when running a business? Cash flow? Sales? Accounting? Competition? Staffing? Growth? Margins?

The answer is all of them, except you can't deal with everything at once. The best analogy I can think of is Whack-a-Mole, a game found on carnival midways, where players hover over a dozen or more holes while holding a mallet. In no particular sequence, and without warning, a small, furry creature pops out of one of the holes. Your job is to whack it with the mallet as soon as it appears, then prepare to whack the next furry creature that is sure to pop up in some other hole, totally at random. Whack enough of the little devils at the right time and you win the game.

So be prepared. Always have the mallet in hand and your eye on the game. When a mole or a problem appears, deal with it as quickly and efficiently as possible, then immediately get ready for the next one to pop up.

20

Why It's Hard for Good Soldiers to Make Great Businesspeople

Some business observers preach that successful companies resemble victorious armies, treating markets as battlefields, staff as soldiers, products as armaments and strategies as battle plans. It's a colourful analogy, but not one that I entirely accept.

I support the concept of seeking total victory over the competition. I see no advantage in ceding any portion of the markets my company serves to competitors. Why should I be satisfied with 50 per cent, 75 per cent or even 90 per cent of my target market if 100 per cent is attainable?

Other parallels between business and the military don't hold up either, and I believe I have identified some of the reasons. For example, military training teaches discipline and sacrifice, two admirable qualities for anyone who chooses a business career. So why don't many former soldiers become extraordinary business successes? I suspect it's a matter of pursuing your self-interest versus sacrificing yourself for the greater good. The latter is essential on the battlefield. The former is vital when encouraging exceptional performance from employees.

Both instances involve a need to make sacrifices. Employees may be asked to sacrifice their time with family to ensure that a project is completed and the company's goals are met, and soldiers may be asked to sacrifice their lives for their nation's cause.

I cannot imagine accomplishing anything of value in this world without making some kind of sacrifice. Anyone who is driven to succeed recognizes this fact, and sometimes the most inspiring people you meet are those who not only make the necessary sacrifice, but do so willingly and without complaint.

Making Sacrifices for the Good of Others

During the long periods when my dad was imprisoned for criticizing the communists, my uncle filled the role of father figure to me. His personality and work ethic made an impression on me, and the older I get, the more I admire him.

My uncle was truly the salt of the earth. He'd had a difficult life, scrabbling out a living in the tiny village where I lived for a while with my grandparents. He had little education, simple tastes and limited expectations. But whenever anyone in the village needed assistance of any kind, they knew they could rely on him. Everything my uncle did seemed dedicated to a higher ideal, an opportunity to make things better for everyone around him. I never spent a minute in his presence without feeling that life, as he defined it, is all about giving of yourself to whatever you value.

I admired my uncle, but I am not like him at all. I discovered just how different I am, and how the difference accounts for my business sense, a few years ago when I was invited to attend a training program operated by former U.S. Army Rangers. The location was a rural region in Kentucky, where all the participants would be challenged according to the training that the Rangers underwent.

Army Rangers are the elite of the U.S. military, selected for their exceptional qualities and sent to three different training camps, each dealing with a different aspect of leadership and endurance. Out of maybe a hundred thousand candidates, only two thousand are chosen to be Rangers, based on their outstanding mental and physical characteristics.

The physical demands are extreme: food rations are limited to 2,200 calories daily, and recruits average perhaps three and a half hours of sleep each night. Any excess fat on the trainee's body is quickly burned up with constant long-distance runs, calisthenics, hand-to-hand combat training and other activities. You don't get past the basic Ranger testing phase unless you can perform eighty to one hundred push-ups, a similar number of sit-ups, fifteen to twenty chin-ups and complete a two-mile run in less than thirteen minutes. Then things get tougher—extended marches in army boots with a fifty-pound pack on your back, five-mile runs three or four times a week, and swimming across fast currents while in full uniform.

To put it bluntly, you work your butt off, and the dropout rate is very high. Those who successfully complete the course acquire leadership skills unavailable anywhere else. Most of the dropouts, by the way, do so not because of the physical demands but the mental challenges. I find it interesting that the mind will often give up before the body does. (When I run a marathon, for instance, it is not my body that gives out, but my mind's ability to believe that my body can keep going.)

I attended the school not as a recruit intent on a military career—the Ranger school replicates some of the training without being affiliated with the military—but because I'd been invited. I thought it would be an interesting experience that might help me improve my leadership skills.

Even the process of reaching the Ranger training facility was challenging. You fly into a remote area of Kentucky and drive for three hours through the backwoods, where you meet some former Army Rangers who will control your life for the next four days. One of the premises of the camp concerns food. You will be given a mission to accomplish, you are informed. Complete your mission successfully and you get to eat. Fail to complete your mission and you don't eat. It's as simple, direct and rigid as that.

Self-Interest vs. Self-Sacrifice

Ranger training is as much psychological as it is physical. For example, before leaving for the camp, you are told to bring items with you that you might wish to have along for comfort of one kind or another. Some people brought instant coffee, others brought grooming utensils or similar items. As soon as we arrived at the camp, everything was taken from us. I grasped the process immediately: we were about to be broken down, then rebuilt into someone quite different from the person we were when we arrived.

We weren't subjected to anything like the full training that real Rangers undergo, but a good deal of the experience over the four days concentrated on developing and sharpening our leadership skills. At one point I had a question for one of the Rangers conducting the training, and his answer provided the content for this chapter.

"How is it," I asked, "that you are so successful at creating leadership skills here, yet so few Rangers become business leaders? Why can't everyone who achieves Ranger status in the army transfer those same skills to the corporate world and become outstanding CEOs?"

The answer had nothing to do with leadership training, and everything to do with personal motivation. Military professionals, I was told, do not focus on personal achievements the way businesspeople do. Instead, they have a need to contribute beyond themselves. Army leadership is all about making sacrifices for the greater good, which means whatever objective their country is aiming towards.

Almost every objective in business is restricted to the good of the corporation and, especially in sales, to the good of the individual. Achieving corporate goals may address "the greater good" of the corporation, but to the trained military mind, selling more widgets is not easily comparable to defending the nation. When a sales manager orders one of his team to become more effective in order to reach that month's quota, it's very different from a sergeant ordering a platoon member to attack a position during combat.

Much military training is based on self-sacrifice at various levels. You sacrifice your civilian freedom for military discipline, you give up a normal family life to be posted overseas, and you risk your own life to carry out orders in combat situations. If you cannot accept these aspects of military life, you're in the wrong profession.

That's hardly the way with sales, or with becoming a successful entrepreneur. Both are based not on self-sacrifice but on self-interest.

My uncle fought in the vicious civil war that tore his country apart, and he managed to survive. Had he been born in the U.S., he might have qualified for Ranger training—he's that tough and dedicated. But he could not have launched a company like mine and built it into an operation valued at more than $100 million. To do so required, among other qualities, enormous self-interest. The greater good may indeed be addressed by some businesses but, like the money generated by my firm when I sold it, it is a by-product of realizing a dream.

21

When Necessary, Burn the Ships

All traditional business books emphasize the importance of leadership. No organization can hope to succeed if the people at the top are incapable of leading employees towards a shared vision. Outstanding leadership, however, isn't based entirely on being able to create brilliant strategies or making great decisions on matters dealing with design, financing, distribution, pricing, expansion or other tangible matters.

The most influential quality of great business leaders has less to do with leading an organization than with *inspiring* it.

Help Others Meet Their Goals

While my experience at the army camp showed me the limits of military training in assisting business decisions, I recognized that the Ranger training philosophy had a few things in common with my approach to management. Running around the country with a fifty-pound pack on your back wasn't one of them. It was the choice to inspire people rather than lead them.

I don't want to lead people anywhere. Leading people suggests I have a rope around their neck and they're following me as I drag them along. It's far more efficient to inspire people to the same level of passion for whatever you are doing as you have yourself. One way to achieve this is by making the people you depend upon feel important. I've been able to do this by asking questions about them, their work and their family. People respond in a positive manner to those who express interest in their lives, and someone who achieves that kind of response can serve as an inspiration.

Those with the knack to inspire their people, rather than ordering or leading them, discover their organizations are capable of achieving goals that appeared beyond their capabilities in the past. That knack, by the way, is much more common among entrepreneurs than among managers.

Of course, you'll never inspire people unless they are convinced you know where you're going. So it's necessary to keep checking your compass, the one that pointed you towards launching your business in the first place. In the beginning, there will be many distractions caused by unforeseen events that may involve financing, competition, the economy, technological developments or a host of other areas. When these occur, pause long enough to recall your original goal, and confirm that you're still heading towards it. If not, change direction or establish a new goal.

Can you create a new goal? Do you know why it must be changed? Do you know how to reach it? And, most critically, can you inspire your employees to visualize the new goal and work effectively to reach it?

Let's Hear It for Hernándo!

It's human nature to resist change, especially when the change involves your source of income and much of your identity. Unless the need is dramatic and self-evident—a barbarians-at-the-gate kind of crisis—many members of an organization will pay lip service to the idea of change while finding ways to cling to the same familiar routine. Unless they can be persuaded to commit entirely to the steps needed for change, a corporate plan risks failure.

As an executive responsible for effecting the necessary change, you may be tempted to implement a range of tactics, from cajoling and rewarding to threatening and intimidating. Few will be effective, in my experience. In times where a crisis-driven change is needed, I like to recall Hernándo Cortez.

You may remember the story of Cortez from your history lessons; he and a few hundred men conquered the Aztec nation that had, for centuries, dominated the Yucatán region of what is now Mexico. Despite being outnumbered by a hundred to one by some estimates, the Spaniards achieved victory thanks to their leader's audacity in ensuring that everyone in his party was as dedicated to victory as he was.

Cortez believed that he and his men would defeat the Aztec nation no matter the odds. The challenge, of course, was to inspire the same confidence in his followers. It would be a difficult achievement, so Cortez didn't even try. Instead of building confidence in his men, he injected them with desperation. It was a stroke of twisted inspiration.

After landing at Yucatán in early 1519, Cortez ordered all the soldiers, sailors and horses off the eleven ships that had carried them there from Cuba, and set fire to every vessel. "If we are going home," Cortez reportedly told his men, "we are going home in *their* ships."

That's an extreme approach to inspiring your team. The Spaniards couldn't retreat, nor could they surrender. If they wanted to survive and see their families again, they had only one choice: win.

If you're serious about starting your own business, give this strategy a lot of thought. Are you totally confident in your ability to achieve success? Will you put every effort behind the new business, and sink or swim according to your energy, determination and ability?

Not giving yourself a fallback position if things don't go as planned takes a good deal of confidence and commitment, which is just what you need when starting a business. The less commitment you give it, the less chance you have of succeeding.

Be prepared to burn your ships.

22

Don't Bank on the Banks

Business doesn't get done without credit. Neither, for that matter, does much in modern life in general. This means we must deal with banks, an action that makes many people nervous and disheartened. It also means drafting business plans to explain your company's operations and future goals. Of all the demands placed on businesspeople, especially those running start-up companies, dealing with banks and drafting business plans are two of the least enjoyable.

Banks Want to Be Your Lender, Not Your Partner

Banks love to market themselves as being your partner in business. The idea of having a partner with billions of dollars in assets may give you a warm, fuzzy feeling, but it's not really true. The role of a bank is not to be a venture capitalist or a business partner; it's to lend money that is expected to be paid back with added interest, which represents the bank's profit.

That's their business. Your business, I expect, is quite differ-ent in nature. So how can you be partners? The bank may mon-itor your progress and confirm the state of the assets securing their loan, but it won't be there to help you resolve an overnight production crisis or develop a brilliant new marketing strategy. That's your job, not theirs.

Time and again, I see a parallel between the difficulty that some businesspeople seem to have with banks and the disastrous pitches made to us on *Dragons' Den*. The problems are invari-ably rooted in a failure among business owners to understand the interests of the source of financing, as well as to communicate their needs effectively.

Remember that the bank's business is to recover the money it lends, along with the interest accrued. If there is no guarantee of recovering the money, the interest charged is irrelevant. That's why banks make such an effort to assess the security of their loans. This upsets many entrepreneurs, who believe the banks simply fail to appreciate the potential of their business. I understand and sympathize with them, but whenever I hear someone grumble that their bank demanded personal guarantees and collateral before granting a loan, my question to them is, "If you were the bank, would *you* lend the money without that kind of assurance?"

On *Dragons' Den*, we're not bankers but we are a source of financing, so we naturally share the same concerns as banks. Chief among these are "How do we get our money back?" and "How much profit can we make along the way?" I'm convinced that the same glaring errors made by many of the pitchers on the shows are also made when many new businesspeople approach banks for funding.

How to Get Financing

Granted, *Dragons' Den* is intentionally far more theatrical than a bank loan manager's office, but in many ways it's a matter of degree. Whether you approach a bank for funding or make a pitch on *Dragons' Den,* you increase your chances of success enormously by following a few rules.

- **Know your facts.** I'm amazed how little research has been done by many people who seek money to fund their businesses. If you're a potential manufacturer, you must know your cost of production, your wholesale margin and the expected retail price, along with your primary competitor's position. Every business operates in a market, so you need to determine the size of the market, whether it is expanding or shrinking, and so on. When seeking funds, you should know these facts as well as you know your own name.

- **You have ninety seconds.** You may have heard of the "elevator pitch." Meaning that, if you can't make your point persuasively in the time it takes an elevator to travel three floors, you've lost the chance to make an impact. On *Dragons' Den* you have perhaps a minute and a half to capture our undivided attention. If we're not engaged in your idea by then, you have lost us. Timing is not as critical when dealing with banks, but the premise still applies: seize the other person's attention from the beginning.

- **Communicate effectively.** Facts and figures are important, but they are not the only criteria. In addition to having the facts in your head and on paper, you must present them in a manner that generates confidence. Speak directly and convincingly. Control your nervousness. Watch your body language.
- **Value your company realistically.** Confidence and dreams are wonderful things, but they hold limited value for a banker or investor. The biggest obstacle encountered by pitchers on *Dragons' Den* is the unrealistic valuations they place on their companies.
- **Understand relative value.** One of the things I always tell pitchers is that the value of their business is related to the value of others in a similar field. If I go into a neighbourhood to buy a house, and someone tells me the house is worth $1.5 million, the first thing I do is find out what other homes in the area have sold for. It's the same for the value of your company: if you think it's worth $10 million, show me examples of similar companies that sold for that. Even then, your company may not be worth that much.
- **Know the goldern rule:** a thing is only worth what someone is willing to pay for it.
- **The only measure of success is sales.** If your business is already in operation, what is your sales volume? Sales are tangible proof that your vision is real. Promises don't count—if you haven't made any sales yet, you haven't justified an investment.
- **Define your share of the market, not the size of the market.** One of the things pitchers do that irritates me most is mention what we Dragons call "The 1% Market." They'll come on

the show and tell us the market is worth, say, $10 billion, and if they can only get one per cent of that, well . . . I don't care how big the market is. I'm interested in how you are going to capture a share—any share—of that market.

- **Don't underestimate your role.** Banks and investors base their decisions to provide funds on two things: the nature of the business and the quality of the person running it. You may believe the facts speak for themselves, but they rarely do; they need the businessperson to speak for them.

The Limits of Business Plans

One of the problems I have with traditional management techniques concerns business plans. I understand business plans; I think they're fine for some situations, but rarely for mine. To me, a business plan is like a weather forecast—it's useful and accurate for the next hour or so, questionable in its value for tomorrow and pure speculation for a week from now.

The businesses I have founded and operated defy the logic of business plans because both they and the industry they serve keep reinventing themselves. The industry is constantly expanding in unpredictable directions, and you have to be prepared to either zig or zag depending on which way it's headed. You rarely have much time to react, let alone consult your business plan and decide on a new strategy. So why spend time drafting a business plan that you know will be obsolete almost before you can implement it?

Because it imposes discipline on your thinking. It also forces you to consider the chasm between your business plan and reality. No matter how realistic you may feel you are being in drafting projections for your company today, reviewing it a year from now will likely be a revelation. I prepare annual business plans for my company not because the banks demand it but because it measures how accurately I can project future developments. Sometimes I'm disappointed at my accuracy and sometimes I am pleasantly surprised. Either way, it connects my galloping ambition with hard reality, and that's good.

I wish the pitchers on *Dragons' Den* were more attuned to that fact. Optimism is wonderful, but reality is truth. Sometimes truth can be cold, hard and unforgiving, but it is always real.

One pitcher on *Shark Tank* sold us on investing in his company, subject to due diligence. Upon closer inspection, we discovered that his business plan predicted sales would grow from zero to $500,000 in the first year, to $5 million by the second year, and $30 million by the end of the third year.

"Do you realize," I asked him, "that you would be one of the most successful companies in history if you achieved these sales figures?"

He was surprised. He assumed, perhaps, that all companies had a good chance of generating $30 million in sales within their first three years. On that basis alone, I withdrew from the deal.

The Rush of Uncertainty

Among all the differences between entrepreneurs and the professionals they must deal with—including bankers, accountants and lawyers—none is more dramatic than the way each deals with uncertainty. Bankers, accountants and lawyers crave stability and predictability; entrepreneurs thrive on chaos. In my case, not knowing what is about to happen generates all the adrenalin I need.

If I knew precisely how many new contracts and projects I would have next month or next year, as well as the customer's names and their needs, I'm not sure I would race to the office every morning. The thing that gets me leaping out of bed before dawn is this idea of uncertainty, of knowing that my staff and I may have to deal with something we hadn't faced before, throwing ourselves wholeheartedly into it and moving on to a new crisis tomorrow or the next day.

On several occasions, my wife, Diane, has asked about the status of some calamity that preoccupied me a week earlier, and it has taken me a few minutes to recall what it was and how it was resolved because I had encountered two or three since. I had honestly forgotten about the crisis that was foremost in my mind just a few days before. This endless chain of potential disasters would drive some people mad, or at least out of the business. I happen to love it.

So how do I deal with people who find this business style upsetting, all those bankers and other bottom line–fixated folk? By reminding myself that they don't really care about my company or me—not on a basic level. They're looking out for their own comfort level. When bankers ask, "How's your business going?" the real question behind their words is, "How safe is the money I loaned you, and will I get in trouble for having advanced it?" An accountant's similar question may mean, "Were you hiding anything from me when I completed your annual report and showed the firm is in good shape?"

Whenever questions like these come up, my standard response is, "Things are fine, we're on target with our plan and we expect to hit our projected growth for the year." Answers like these are never outright lies; I would never claim that my company was healthy and growing if it were teetering on the brink of bankruptcy. They are phrased, however, to address the concerns of whoever asks the question and leave them feeling comfortable. It follows the rule of knowing how to adapt to different situations.

23

How Less Can Become More

Too many crises and too much chaos can be crippling, not energizing. When this occurs, step away from the confusion for a few moments and review your original goals.

I did this with one of my first companies. The business had grown steadily, if not spectacularly, over the first year of its operation, functioning as a kind of one-stop shopping centre for network access. Then it stopped—not the business, but the growth. In business parlance, we plateaued, and for several months nothing seemed capable of restoring our previous growth levels.

I'm something of a Darwinist where business is concerned. As I stated earlier, **your business either grows or it dies. Expansion isn't a goal or a business strategy. It is an undeniable fact of life.** My business was no longer growing, and I was damned if I was going to watch it die.

I spent a good deal of time asking myself how I could kickstart the company's growth. None of the options I considered— branding or expanding—made sense. If we did those things we would become just another also-ran in a very crowded field, assuming we survived the start-up and development costs.

The answer to restoring growth, I realized, consisted not in expanding into regions where we lacked skills, products and identity but by *reducing* the number of our products and services. Our growth was being stifled not by the number of services we provided but by a lack of intensity in our focus.

Internet security, I recognized, had become a key component of successful networking, and the need would not only be continuous, it would also need constant revisions and updates. Every advance in network security represented another challenge for mischievous hackers and hardened criminals to defeat or sidestep, and their efforts had to be anticipated and derailed. Computer network security wasn't like installing a bank vault that would sit in place for decades, protecting its contents with steel and concrete. It was a form of choreography, a constantly moving and evolving dance whose steps were both logical *and* unpredictable. It was also a growing aspect of business, one that would easily outpace the rapid evolution of computer hardware in market value.

We needed to focus our energy and attention on becoming a network security specialist, poised to lead the industry in that sector.

I divested the company of everything and everyone not directly associated with delivering network security solutions, narrowing our focus and sharpening our intensity. It worked. Within weeks our growth began a hockey stick–like ascent, leading us to revenue and profit levels that surprised even me.

In this case, the secret to growth was not to expand the roster of products and services, but to refocus, in the process identifying a market we could lead and eventually dominate. It's a variation on the design concept that less is more. In this case, more can be less if the more prevents you from focusing on the things you and your organization do best. It's better to do two or three things very well than to do a dozen things in a merely passable manner. This represents a lesson, I believe, that remains to be learned by many giant multinational corporations, as well as by small start-up firms grappling with the challenge of growth.

Remember that growth is measurable. Track improvements in your sales and profit levels often—they are the only true test of your company's success. Set goals for your firm's growth. When you hit or exceed them, celebrate and aim higher. When you miss them, determine why and fix the problem. Above all, don't make excuses.

You can't ignore reality, however, and reality says that markets can decline, never to rise to their previous levels. If this is responsible for your lack of growth, don't attempt to revive your fortunes or aim for a larger share of a dying market. Cut your losses and move on.

Diane's List of Things That Make Me Successful

I asked my wife, Diane, for a list of the qualities that, in her view, lie behind my success in business. Following are her responses (in no particular order).

- **You are adaptable.** You have no problem changing direction suddenly when you need to. In fact, I suspect you enjoy it.
- **When you focus on a problem, you are relentless in pursuing the solution.**
- **You can detach your emotion from the situation and become all business when required.**
- **You are very good at defining the end result you want and figuring out how to get there.**
- **You know when you need a break from business, and you take it (but it's always brief).**
- **You have a chip on your shoulder, and the attitude keeps driving you to be better than others.**
- **You seek the opinions of others and take them seriously.** (You proved it by asking me to do this!)
- **You want to learn from others who can pass their wisdom on to you.**
- **You don't dwell on your mistakes; you acknowledge them and move on quickly.**
- **You married me.**

24

Prepare to Wear the Black Hat

Driven as I am, it's no hardship for me to be in the office hours before anyone else. In fact, were it not for obligations to my family I would gladly spend twenty-four hours a day in my office, getting things done. If you're driven to succeed, you understand that. If you're not, perhaps you never will.

The joy of my job, of course, comes from building things, from elevating the level of my company's success to new heights. That's what makes the adrenalin flow, and in the middle of all these accomplishments my employees and I can share the warm glow and good feelings they bring. We're all heroes. We all wear white hats, like the good guys in old western movies.

When challenges are faced on a minor scale, like informing an employee that he or she no longer has a job with my company, I can still play the role of the good guy because I can take the time to do it as fairly and gently as possible.

Sometimes, however, the problem is so immense and serious that widespread action must be taken, affecting scores of people in order to save the corporation. No matter how much you tell yourself you're still a good guy for saving some of the jobs instead of losing all of them, it's difficult to pretend your hat is anything but black in colour. This may, in fact, be the biggest challenge you face as a businessperson.

First, You Hit Rock Bottom

A friend of mine once suggested that businesses in serious trouble are like people with a crippling long-term addiction to drugs or alcohol. No matter how much you try to help them, they need to reach rock bottom before they can start rising again.

None of the companies I launched came near to hitting the bottom, but I nevertheless acquired some painful experience in one turnaround strategy.

After I gained some notoriety through the sale of my company to AT&T, a friend called me from Silicon Valley in California, first congratulating me on the sale, then challenging my business ability. "You're pretty hot stuff in Canada," he said. "How well do you think you would be playing among the big boys in Silicon Valley?" He had something specific in mind: he owned a substantial number of shares in a troubled company similar to mine and was spearheading efforts to save it.

I knew the company well. I also knew that, barely a year earlier, its founder had turned down a purchase offer of $870 million, insisting on a price of $1 billion because that was the amount some friends had received a few weeks earlier for their company. Shortly after that decision, the dot-com bubble burst, the company's financial problems became critical and, as a result, it risked being delisted from the Nasdaq stock exchange.

"In theory," my friend asked when I had a handle on the scope of the company's problems, "what would you do to save the company, assuming it can be saved at all?"

I replied that the solution was clear, but the cure would be painful. The size of the product line would have to be reduced, excess inventory would have to be sold at a discount, the company had to refocus itself and the workforce had to shrink drastically in size.

"You've got it," my friend said. "Think you can do it?"

Thus began one of the most challenging periods in my life. Building companies from the ground up had been the secret of my success and the source of my joy in work. Now I would be tearing down an existing company, headquartered in a strange location, stripping enough flab to enable it to rise and function in a leaner and, if necessary, meaner fashion.

Essentially, I operated as the company's hatchet man. Eliminating jobs and cancelling projects that people may have worked on for years is a difficult chore for anyone, and it was especially tough for me. I soon took the attitude of a surgeon amputating a limb to save a patient. The action may be both painful and tragic, but it was more important to lose part of the body than lose it all. If the company died, everyone's job would be eliminated. If I could help it survive, at least 20 per cent of the staff would keep their jobs. That was the mantra I kept repeating through all the pain I knew I was causing many people.

In a word, I crushed the company, stripping it to its core of employees, products and operations. It took a year and a half to shape the company into one whose bottom line turned from red to black and whose share price multiplied six times between the day I arrived and when I departed. By then, a major international corporation had made a healthy offer to purchase it, and my role as a hatchet man ended, a source of great relief for me and my family.

I do not hope to ever repeat those events but, like every new business experience, this one brought some special lessons with it.

Major Problems Rarely Fix Themselves

It's routine to compare corporations with living organisms, and the analogy can be valuable when diagnosing problems. In the same way our own bodies tackle the common cold, some corporate problems can cure themselves of mild afflictions. But serious illness can't be ignored in our bodies or in the companies we manage. Ignore either long enough and the result is almost always fatal.

Using the same analogy, the sooner a serious disease is diagnosed, the more effective the cure, so we should be on the lookout for symptoms and address them accordingly. Many symptoms are easy to ignore in a small business, where cash flow may be a continuous and more immediate problem. There must be a limit, in time or extent, beyond which you can no longer ignore the symptoms listed below.

Five Serious Symptoms of Trouble

1. A constant shortage of cash to pay all bills in full when they become due.
2. A reliance on bank loans and overdrafts to keep the company solvent (it's one thing to be short of cash because

you're growing like crazy; quite another because you are borrowing to fund operations).

3. A dramatic reduction in the owner's (or proprietor's or shareholders') income and profits.
4. A constant concern about potential failure.
5. An inability to reduce the company's debt position.

When drastic action is needed, the big solutions may appear obvious—cut expenses, grow margins, reduce staff and inventory, and so on. All well and good. But executing them awkwardly or ineffectively may backfire, creating an entirely new range of legal, financial and image problems that, instead of saving the corporation, could doom it.

Saving an ailing company, as I discovered, requires a scalpel as much as a hatchet, especially when applied to the steps shown below.

Ten Steps Forward

1. **Stop the bleeding.** A physician encountering a hemorrhaging patient doesn't take time to ask about the individual's diet or whether he or she is a smoker. The overriding concern is to stem the flow of blood, which, if unchecked, will unquestionably prove fatal. When faced with a company in difficulties, the first thing to check is cash flow—is more money leaving the company than entering it? If so, this demands your primary attention. Everything else can wait.
2. **Forget "quick fix" solutions.** Your firm's condition probably did not occur overnight, so don't expect to cure things in the

same time frame. Urgency is necessary, but so is a long-term strategy to prevent a recurrence and get the company back on solid footing. The best plan: separate short-term actions (immediate cost reductions) from long-term needs (new products or services) and manage them in parallel.

3. **Do not delegate.** This is not the time for macromanagement, but for micromanagement on your part. Saving the company is your responsibility, and all actions should be made with your direct authority. This may not be the "normal" way of running your company, but the situation should not be considered normal. Don't count on your current management team to solve things on their own; if they had been effective, you wouldn't be facing the crisis in the first place.

4. **Make a clear distinction between turnaround expenses and operating expenses.** You cannot track the effectiveness of your turnaround program unless you can measure the cost accurately. For example, salaries and severance pay for laid-off personnel should be plotted separately from the cost of keeping the company afloat.

5. **Don't try to hide the urgency; proclaim it.** You have two incentives to follow this advice. First, you can create a positive team atmosphere—not panic—by creating the attitude that "We're all in this together" and helping everyone stay on message. Second, if layoffs are necessary, there may be legal requirements to alert personnel to the possibility.

6. **Manage up if necessary.** Shareholders, financiers and parent-company executives need to be apprised of the situation in a factual manner.

7. **Identify and nurture your most profitable products or services.** They may surprise you. For example, your most profitable sections may not represent your core business; in any case, they do represent your best source of badly needed income and deserve attention.

8. **Find the niche where you can be number one.** This means narrowing your focus over and over again if necessary. Becoming the dominant player in your market is the best way to create stability.

9. **Know the biggest source of savings on employee salaries.** It's middle managers. Look for inefficiency levels here first, and take necessary action.

10. **Expect to win.** If you were driven to create the company, you have the drive to rescue it. Keep reminding yourself that failure is just part of the game, and the only way you can be defeated is by quitting.

25

How to Play Hardball Without Feeling Bad

Within the limits of the law and standards of decency, every business has the right to eliminate its competitors by offering better value, performance and service. It's easier to do this when a company employs a team of skilled people sharing the same goal and powered by the same enthusiasm. And if you believe in the axiom "Keep growing or die," that attribute is a necessity.

Managing and building a business requires you to be ruthless with your competitors and severe with your own people from time to time. This can be a challenge to some people, even those determined to achieve the highest level of success available to them. Some people find it easy to make unpopular decisions. Others, including me, have to learn the trick for themselves.

Everyone loves to feel loved, and not every decision we make is guaranteed to generate fondness for us in the hearts of those affected by it. So how to cope? You look beyond the immediate impact of your decision. If you are firing someone, for example, you need to be confident that your decision is in the best interests of the organization, and perhaps even in the best interests of the employee you're dismissing. That's not an ironic comment. Many people, including me, look back on the trauma of losing a job with the realization that it was one of the most beneficial events in their careers.

You Don't Have to Eliminate Your Competitor, but You Should Want To

You can find motivation to make harsh decisions in various places besides, of course, the need to grow, revive or even rescue your business. Mine is based, I believe, in the fact that I grew up in a loving home environment.

My mother's loving manner balanced a lot of everyday cruelty I experienced as a child who understood little English, wore highly unfashionable clothes, and simply didn't fit in. Her message to me was this: It may be a rough and unfair world out there, but within our own small world—the apartment I shared with my parents—nothing mattered as long as we could control who we were, what we did and what we would accomplish. Later, when I began wrestling in the often down-and-dirty world of business, the memory of my mother's words helped me make decisions that were tough but warranted, and deflected any guilt and concern I may have had about making them.

Over the years I developed a reputation as being a tough guy in my business dealings. I don't believe I am. But when it comes to making business decisions, I believe this: it's a zero-sum game. For my firm to truly win, our competition has to lose. In the rapidly developing rough-and-tumble world of technology, there is no other way of doing business.

I know it's fashionable to talk about win-win situations these days. That may work in a marriage, but marriage isn't a competition (or shouldn't be), it's a relationship. I have no relationship with my competitors. I may have a relationship with their top executives or other members of the company, whom I may like and admire as individuals. But I have no affection for the organizations, nor do I expect their managers to have any affection for my own. As competitors battling each other for the same dollars spent by the same customers in the same market, we are adversaries whose existence threatens and inhibits the others.

When I purchased a company several years ago and reviewed its accounts list, I commented to one of the managers about the presence of a highly regarded multinational firm. "That's a good customer to have on our list," I said.

"Yeah," the manager replied. "We're happy we have part of their business."

"Happy with just part?" I responded. "Why don't we have all the business?"

"Well, we have a deal with our competitor," the manager explained. "We do this part of the business, they handle the other part, and this way we don't step on each other's toes."

I took a minute to absorb this, then told all the managers in the room: "Everybody listen carefully to me. We are going after all the business we can get from this customer, and we'll keep doing it until the other guys are gone. I don't care if this means putting them out of business. We'll do it."

The managers were not pleased with my comment. In fact, they were worried. "What if the other guys go after *our* business?" one of them said.

I told him I could not possibly care less. "If we can't stand on our own value proposition to this client," I said, "we don't deserve their business. And if we can't do the same with all our customers, we don't deserve to be in business at all."

This decision was made not only to benefit us, but ultimately to benefit the customer as well. As long as we remained comfortable with just a portion of the customer's business, we would never stretch ourselves. When we determined to take the other guy's part of the business away from him, we wouldn't base it on customer loyalty. We would do it by delivering better quality, better service and better value to the customer. That way, we would improve the customer's situation as well as our own. One of the partners in the process—our competitor—might lose, but the other two would win. Two winners out of three players—hey, what's wrong with that?

Tony Blair's Guide to Leadership

Former British prime minister Tony Blair is one of the most engaging men you could encounter. I met and chatted with him a few years ago and, while he's not quite up to former U.S. president Bill Clinton's level of amiable charm, Blair remains a man with a remarkable grasp of global enterprise.

Here's a quotation of his that I admire a great deal: "The art of leadership is the ability to say no."

I appreciate those words because the ability to say no at the right time to the right person in the right way was one of the most difficult skills I had to learn in business. For a very long time, my response to a suggestion or proposal I disagreed with was to mouth a version of "maybe," which simply bought time. Now I try to say no where it's appropriate.

Learn how to say no when you need to, because your customers, your bank and your suppliers will all say it when *they* need to.

Remember Where Your Prime Responsibility Lies

As my company grew, it was inevitable that some people joining it lacked the same drive and focus that I had, a fact that was difficult for me to accept. I had no patience with employees who lacked that quality, even as I realized it was impossible for everyone to share it. If I couldn't inject the same degree of enthusiasm I felt in working for the company into the veins of my employees, I would have to create it in other ways, which usually worked. When it failed to succeed, I chose to end their careers with my firm.

This wasn't easy for me. I suspect it's not easy for anyone, and firing someone may well be the most difficult action anyone in an executive position must take. It doesn't help to tell the newly unemployed person it's necessary, or that in future years they may look back and realize it was the best thing that happened to them. When you are looking someone in the eye and are about to tell them that they are no longer employed, no longer drawing a salary, no longer going to work among people who have become their friends, and no longer can harbour whatever dreams they may have of rising within your organization—well, it's almost as painful for you as it is for them, sometimes more. The only comfort you can take is that very few people who must handle that chore find it easy—even a battlefield commander.

When he was retiring, former U.S. Army General Norman Schwarzkopf was asked to name any errors he had made in his distinguished career. "My biggest mistake," the general replied, "was to keep people I personally liked in positions where they were incompetent. The cost of that mistake was human life." If a tough soldier who watched people die on a battlefield couldn't overcome his personal feelings when dismissing someone who wasn't up to the job, you probably won't find it any easier to fire an employee.

The best way to prepare yourself for the process of firing someone is to remind yourself where your first responsibility lies. It's not with you personally and it's not with the employee you are about to terminate. Your first responsibility is to the company.

Corporations are living, breathing entities, and the company has to survive at all costs. If you are unable to move someone who cannot perform his or her job out of that position—and, if necessary, out of the company itself—you risk the health of the corporation. Firing people when absolutely necessary requires an acquired skill just like any other management talent, except that this one also may involve growing a thicker skin.

Knowing these things didn't always make it easy. In some cases it didn't make me any friends either. I'm a social guy who enjoys the company of friends and employees as much as anyone, assuming they don't interfere with business. But I couldn't afford to worry about the reactions of others to my decisions, and frankly I didn't. Much of this was linked to the solid family values I learned as a child, especially the confidence borne of being appreciated by my family. Whatever feelings my actions might have generated in my business, I was loved by people at the core of my life. This knowledge, and the intangible warmth it provided, helped make me a better businessman—as, I assume, it helps everyone else in a similar position.

Hire Slowly, Fire Quickly

Here's the difficult dichotomy of running a business: telling someone they have a job and then watching their reaction is fun, so you look forward to doing it as quickly as possible; telling someone they are unemployed and then experiencing their disappointment is painful, so you want to put it off. Unfortunately, both reactions are in opposition to logic.

Even for the most basic tasks, it costs money to train a new employee. If the employee is not suitable for the position because you made your decision too quickly, it will cost your company needlessly. A little more time to ensure you have chosen the perfect person for the job reduces the likelihood of wasting money in that fashion. At the other end, paying salaries or wages to someone who is not performing satisfactorily represents another blow to your bottom line. The longer he or she stays on the job, the more money you're pouring down the drain, so why delay? Death is almost always fatal. You need to live in order to fight another day.

Do's and Don'ts of Dismissing Employees

Do alert the employee to problems with his or her work, giving them an opportunity to correct things.

Do give the decision a lot of thought; once a decision has been made, take action.

Do ensure that legal requirements are met; discuss terms with your lawyer if necessary.

Do prepare a termination letter detailing the terms of the dismissal.

Do be respectful of the employee's dignity and feelings in the meeting.

Do be human about it. You're not discarding a piece of equipment, after all. You are altering the course of a person's life.

Do remind yourself that the company's welfare is being served.

Don't make a decision to fire someone without objective and confirmable information; relying on rumour or individual opinions can be disastrous.

Don't make the reasons personal; keep them business-based.

Don't inform the employee of your decision in a public location or anywhere other employees can learn what is happening.

Don't be unprepared; have your papers ready and rehearse your words.

Don't become defensive or argumentative; confirm that your decision is final.

Don't blame yourself for the decision; if you have been totally honest about things, you didn't fail the employee—the employee failed you.

26

Recognize the ABCs of MBAs

Can you acquire knowledge and skills that will make your business function better from books and classroom studies? Yes. Will this make you a more effective entrepreneur? Not necessarily.

There are many times when you want the sharply focused vision of a specialist. From fixing the plumbing in your house to undergoing surgery, you want someone in charge whose focus and experience have been directed specifically towards the job in hand—making sure your toilets flush well and your appendix comes out cleanly.

And then there are times when you need a wider angle, the view of a generalist who can quickly assess a complex situation and know almost instinctively what needs to be done—not *how* to do it; *why* to do it.

Evening the Odds of Ten Against Ten Thousand

Whenever I talk about making a business pitch against companies ten times our size, I'm asked if we have a secret for matching them with all the show-biz elements—the charts, graphs, video presentations and stagecraft—that every serious business pitch seems to depend upon.

The answer is no, we don't have a secret. In fact, we rarely use any of those devices in our presentations, because we would come out second best.

All the major corporations in our field have access to creative talent and equipment that would impress most Hollywood studios these days. They can afford it. We can't. Producing presentations with a slickness that would look good on Broadway isn't our business, so why try to impress customers with it? Time and effort spent on presentations that might make us look like Warner Brothers is time and effort not invested in selling our strengths.

When your army has ten soldiers and you're battling an enemy of ten *thousand,* it doesn't make sense to spend a lot of time and effort on colourful banners and rehearsing the marching band. You'd better focus on getting a concentrated effort out of everybody on your side, and that's precisely what we do.

This idea of constantly playing the role of underdog is entirely the opposite of the mentality fostered by big corporations a generation ago. I can remember when a group of executives, sales staff or service technicians from a particular company arriving at a customer's offices were greeted as if a pope or president of a foreign country were arriving. I'm not suggesting that the customer's employees bowed and scraped as royalty passed through the reception area, but there was a clear sense that whatever problem the customer faced was about to be solved. This company had earned that respect, of course, and continued to do so. But how do you overcome that kind of competitor's advantage when it comes to soliciting business? The solution defines the difference between entrepreneurs and managers. The latter tends to apply MBA methods.

The classic MBA approach identifies specific issues and searches for ways to counter the competition's advantage. Their price is lower? Sell greater value through service or warranty. Their equipment is faster? Promote extended life, easier installation, cheaper upgrades, whatever. Their marketing budget is bigger? Sharpen the target of your advertising and promotion expenditure to make every dollar work harder.

Business graduates are good at defining problems and proposing solutions when dealing with competitive situations. Their general abilities extend well beyond this topic to include such concerns as accounting, corporate strategy, economics, finance, organizational behaviour, supply chain management and a raft of other topics that make corporate directors, investors and middle managers feel good. I congratulate every successful MBA graduate and admire both their intelligence and perseverance in completing their studies. But frankly, I'm not impressed with their degrees. An individual's passion and inherited abilities are, in many cases, more important than the degree they earn.

The creative talent is the real measure. Bottling, labelling, pricing, shipping and marketing are important stages to a wine company. But the true value of the business, the make-or-break element, depends on the passion and talents of the winemaker, the person at the creative level. Without him or her, the rest of the stuff isn't going to happen.

You obtain an MBA because you want to manage. And you can only manage what already exists.

27

Put Your Money on the Driven Businessperson

Are there two kinds of driven people who choose to become successful in business? I suspect this is true. While most of the skills to launch and successfully manage a business can be acquired, some people appear to be born with them, which provides them with a head start over those who need formal schooling to prepare themselves.

It takes energy and purpose to acquire an MBA, either as an extension of your basic college education or in mid-career, and I admire those who achieve it in either time frame. But what about those who can't stand to postpone their entry into business, especially one they have launched to fulfill their own vision? How do you compare their energy and purpose with the "Gotta get my MBA!" crowd?

Perhaps you can't. Perhaps this really does define two very different approaches to the same goal.

When the Odds Are Twenty to One, I'll Take the Long Shot

Driven businesspeople value good managers, but having them on staff is not why they go to work each day. They go to work creating and improving companies for other people to manage. If the other people have a degree, that's fine. If they also share the leader's vision and focus, that's even better. In a crisis-driven business situation, I will pit one entrepreneur with vision and determination against twenty MBA grads and expect the entrepreneur to win. And, in North America, if the entrepreneur is a first-generation immigrant whose family arrived here nearly broke, I'll increase the size of my bet on the entrepreneur.

An outlandish claim? Not in my book. Here are my three reasons to put money on the entrepreneur:

1. **Managers fear chaos.** Entrepreneurs thrive on it. You've probably heard that the Chinese symbol for crisis also represents opportunity. The connection may be news to management types and the general public, but it's common sense to entrepreneurs. Every crisis opens a door to a new product or service, a new demand to be met, a new market to be explored and new profits to be made. When something bursts into flame among a group of MBAs, their reaction is to look for a means of extinguishing it. Not entrepreneurs; they look for marshmallows to roast.

2. **You make more progress acting than reacting.** One of the biggest problems facing CEOs of corporations is maintaining the ability to anticipate and to respond to challenges that they

initially disregard. In the case of large multinational companies, this reflects the "too big to fail" sentiment that has been proven wrong with the spectacular collapse of firms such as Nortel and Lehman Brothers. You don't need such dramatic failure to recognize the danger of this thinking, however. IBM didn't spawn the computer revolution that began thirty years ago; that was launched by two kids named Steve, working out of a garage in a small California town. Around the same time, people were snickering over the efforts of Honda and Toyota to challenge General Motors for command of the North American automotive market, and retail sales in Canada were dominated by the T. Eaton Company, a venerable and supposedly invincible firm. In these and many other instances, dramatic change occurred when someone recognized the potential offered by new technology and changing buying habits, acted in anticipation of events instead of reacting to competitive challenges, and set unique standards for performance that changed the very nature of the market. Problems for the established companies began when each believed its position was unassailable, and their experiences provide a lesson for every business, regardless of size or industry.

3. **You can be taught to read, but you can't be taught to improvise.** Most truly serious business problems tend to be unique in character. They also tend to be urgent, which means they won't be solved by striking committees, reviewing alternatives or consulting case studies in textbooks. Most are solved by improvising on the spot, a talent that may be learned but can't be taught—it's instinctive and usually driven by a desperate need to succeed.

During the first year or so of running my own company, I improvised all over the place. Would I have performed better with a business degree? I'm not sure. In fact, had I known then as much as I know now about standard business practice, I might not have launched the business at all. Steve Jobs, Steve Wozniak, and Bill Gates didn't earn MBAs. What does that tell you?

I have hired MBA graduates, and I've been glad I did. When things are less dynamic and more reflective—say, when you're assessing the value of a going concern that you are planning to either acquire or sell—the same business-school discipline that keeps getting in the way when you're starting a new company becomes valuable when you're confronting hard facts, especially those churned out on balance sheets and profit-and-loss statements. And when it comes to negotiations, it helps to have an MBA or two on your side dealing with the MBAs on the other side. They associate with each other. They feel comfortable with each other. They talk the same language, wear the same style of clothes and probably eat the same healthy foods for lunch.

Someone, somewhere has earned an MBA before successfully launching his or her business venture and managed to combine these two different approaches in one individual. Whoever it is, I offer my congratulations. In my experience, however, he or she remains the exception that proves the rule.

28

The Quality of Your Performance Depends on the Quality of Your Competition

Few things will make a company flabby, underachieving and ultimately doomed more effectively than weak competitors. Just as good competition delivers better products, service and value to consumers, weak competition creates apathy and atrophy among businesses.

If your business fails to match your expectations, maybe it's because you're not being challenged to perform up to your competitors' level. My advice: go head to head with the very best competitors in your field. Forget the also-rans or the mom-and-pop operations with limited objectives. Aim for the top, and plan to get there one step at a time.

My companies have been successful and profitable, but for various reasons they have not been giants on the same scale as the biggest in the field. Yet if the employees of my companies and I were to make a list of our competitors, all of the top companies would be on that list. They weren't there when we began, with

limited resources and services. Back then, we grew by outper-
forming competitors our own size. But as we built a large enough
roster of clients, we kept setting our sights higher until we could
honestly compete with the very best people in the business and
intentionally target their customers.

Did we win every battle? Hardly, but you never win a game if
you choose not to play. Did competition improve the quality of
our people, products and service? There's no doubt about it.

The best parallel with this strategy I can think of relates to golf.

Despite his recent personal problems, Tiger Woods is clearly
the best professional golfer of his generation, and perhaps the
best in history. He achieved his success by competing not as much
against other golfers as against himself, setting standards that
only he could achieve. Woods and other golfers in his class can
relax when playing a round of golf with Robert Herjavec because,
let's face it, they don't need to be on top of their game to beat me.
Against me, Woods could choose a two-shot to the green and still
feel confident about winning. But he doesn't do that; he can *never*
do that. Competing against himself, he will risk driving the ball
beyond a hazard in a single stroke to the green, because that's the
winning shot. If the toughest competition you face is your own
high standard, you will inevitably become better at your game,
whatever the game may be.

Here's a quick Tiger Woods story to illustrate his obsession
with golf. In the summer of 2009, I accepted an invitation from
Ron Joyce, founder of the Tim Hortons coffee-shop chain, to join
him and some friends at Fox Harb'r, Joyce's luxurious resort on
the north coast of Nova Scotia. The occasion was made especially

memorable by the presence of Tiger Woods, who would play a round on the course with Joyce and his guests.

The event was memorable in many ways. Fox Harb'r may be the most attractive and demanding course on the east coast of North America, laid out in the style of Scotland's St. Andrews. I enjoyed the round and played at my usual level, and of course the highlight was sharing the game with Woods, who may well be the most dominant golfer of his or any generation.

Tiger was impressive, as expected, in his game, but the thing I found most remarkable was the story behind his arrival at Fox Harb'r the evening before.

Fox Harb'r has a first-class airport facility, as well equipped as any in the world considering its size, but Woods was not permitted to land there. The problem wasn't weather; it was insurance restrictions that prohibited any aircraft carrying him from landing at night at an airport where the pilots have not landed in the past. Neither pilot on Woods's plane had been to Fox Harb'r before, so flying Tiger directly there was out of the question. The closest airport where he *was* permitted to land was Halifax, about 150 kilometres to the south.

"No problem," Ron Joyce said when he heard about the situation. "I'll send a helicopter to Halifax for him."

This wouldn't work either. Another clause in Woods's contract says he cannot travel on a helicopter of any size or type for any reason other than a Medevac flight.

So the world's greatest golfer travelled to one of the world's outstanding golf resorts by private bus, arriving at Fox Harb'r sometime after one in the morning. Then, barely four hours after falling into bed, Tiger Woods was in the resort's workout room, running through the same routine he follows day after day, year in and year out. This was followed by an hour or so hitting balls off the tee, all before almost anyone else's day started. Neither the fact that he had undergone a journey that would have tried the most experienced traveller's patience, nor that he was playing a meaningless demonstration round of golf soon after participating in a major tournament, were allowed to interfere with his regimen.

Assessing the Competition

A fundamental flaw shared by many businesspeople is that they don't know what sets their business apart from the competition. It's one thing to say "fluffy" things like "we're better," "we work harder," "our people are better," and on and on. Anyone can do that. But what does it really mean? Do you think the competition has thrown up their hands and said, "We suck—buy from someone else"? You have to know how and why you are better, and be able to quantify it.

The more you know about your competitors' weaknesses, the more effective you can be in avoiding them—or at least in reducing their impact on your own company's success. It's not enough to know who they are and what they do; it's just as important to understand all facets of their operation and choose their weak spots by finding answers to these seven questions.

1. **What is their customer base?** Does it overlap with yours geographically, product-wise and service-wise? In what sectors do you go head to head with them? Are they a niche player?

2. **Why are customers buying from them?** Is it their pricing? Performance? Marketing strategy? Never become so arrogant that you believe there is nothing to learn from your competition.

3. **What financial shape are they in?** Are they stretched to the limit? Flush with cash?

4. **Are they matching supply and demand?** Do they meet their delivery dates? Do they have inventory or supply problems? What is their service record?

5. **Are they expanding or contracting?** Not just geographically, but by product or service.

6. **What do you know of their strategy?** Do they appear content with their current market position? Are they attempting to dominate the market?

7. **Can you measure their resources?** Are they stretched to the limit?

29

Forget a Balanced Life

It would be pleasant to achieve success as an entrepreneur while working 9 to 5 each day and spending undisturbed weekends with family and friends. Unfortunately, that's impossible. The determination of driven businesspeople to succeed overrides personal schedules to the point where it appears obsessive. Obsession needn't be a negative quality, but for those seeking to become rich by launching and operating their own company, it is a necessary one.

People have a totally different attitude towards those who have accumulated wealth through their own efforts. In Eastern Europe, it's widely assumed that anyone who has accumulated substantial wealth did so by ripping people off. You cannot, they believe, make a lot of money without betraying or fleecing someone. In the United States, meanwhile, it's assumed that anyone who has made a lot of money has found a secret to wealth that any other American, with enough luck, energy and determination, can duplicate.

These are generalities, I know, but they reflect contrasting attitudes towards people with large sums of money.

I have a serious problem with the European viewpoint, which also tends to reflect the Canadian outlook. In my experience, an individual's wealth usually has little to do with his or her qualities as a human being. I have encountered wonderfully warm and generous people whose net worth easily exceeds mine, and similar qualities among men and women whose personal possessions were basically the clothes on their back. I have also met scheming, unscrupulous people in both economic camps. The net worth of an individual is never an accurate measure of his or her qualities as a human being.

I can name with total confidence one quality that all successful entrepreneurs share, regardless of the industry they are in or the amount of cash in their savings account: they get very little sleep, compared with other people.

It's not that they suffer from insomnia. They don't "suffer" from anything except determination to achieve success. Nothing gets done when you're sleeping unless you include dreaming, and dreaming rarely produces sales and profits.

When I finally began drawing a salary from the first company I worked for, I spent money on the usual things that a single guy in his twenties finds irresistible—a flashy sports car, nice clothes and a few other luxuries. I had girlfriends and several buddies whose company I enjoyed. When they threw a party, I'd be there. Well, maybe I'd be there.

If something about business occurred that conflicted with a party, the business always won, and I made the decision without a second thought. My workday frequently extended to midnight or beyond, and the next day usually started before 6 a.m. To those who may set their career sights lower than mine, this sounds obsessive. To me, and others like me, it's not obsessive at all. It's necessary.

"Obsessive" has a negative connotation, like a neurosis, the act of someone suffering severe mental problems. I don't believe I have serious mental problems, nor do the various entrepreneurs and highly successful businesspeople I encounter. And I certainly don't believe whatever we "suffer" from represents a negative quality.

The time and effort spent to achieve success is an investment you will never regret making. The memory can even inspire you.

I trained for months before entering my first marathon race in Miami. Finally I was ready and, just before firing the gun, the starter announced to everyone in the race: "Remember: this is the last twenty-six miles you have to run." His words opened a flood of adrenalin and confidence for me. He was correct. I had run a long series of marathons alone in training to prepare for that moment. Now I only had to run one more. I've never forgotten the feeling that announcement created within me. It placed the goal within my reach.

The next time you hear a performance by an exceptional musician, someone with total mastery of his or her instrument, remind yourself that he or she did not play that instrument for the first time last week or last month or even last year. You're not hearing their first or even their tenth performance. It's probably closer to the hundredth or even thousandth time the musician played the music, building the necessary skill and feeling to impress and move you.

The amount of practice it takes to achieve proficiency on a piano, guitar, violin or any other instrument is stunning to non-musicians. In his book *Outliers*, Malcolm Gladwell estimates that it takes ten thousand hours to achieve mastery of a demanding skill, such as becoming a successful recording artist. Eric Clapton once wrote of practising his guitar, alone in his room, twelve hours or more each day, day after day, before he felt good enough to play professionally. Was that obsessive? Eric Clapton fans would shrug and say it didn't matter; they're just glad he chose to do it.

Mick Jagger Is a Rolling Stone

For the very best of their breed, this determination by musicians and performing artists to keep elevating their skills doesn't end with success. On two occasions, Mick Jagger and his family have rented our home while he started rehearsals for Rolling Stone tours. The house is large enough, with all the amenities he appreciates, to accommodate his entourage. It includes a substantial indoor pool and a ballroom with plenty of space for him and his crew to practise their stage moves. Along with exceptional security systems and a somewhat isolated location, our home has everything to make Jagger and his family comfortable.

The first time I encountered Jagger, I was struck by his exceptional physical condition. He carries no excess fat on his body, which is taut, lean and muscular. His lifestyle, I noted, resembled that of an Olympic-level athlete in training rather than a raunchy rock star. Most of his meals included yogurt, whole-grain foods and fresh fruits and vegetables. When I had an opportunity to watch him in rehearsal, I realized that all the moves that keep attracting people to his concerts—the sudden spins, the surprised expressions, the synchronized dance steps—are choreographed and rehearsed over and over until they become automatic, yet they appear completely improvised, which, of course, makes them appealing and entertaining. Whatever public image Jagger has, he maintains his superstar status with a degree of discipline and self-control that could be described as obsessive.

Is there a price for this intense dedication to success? Of course there is. Everything in life has a price, which probably separates winners from losers in business, sports and life itself. If you're not prepared to pay the price, you can't expect to succeed. The price often includes suffering defeat as a result of circumstances or conditions you can't control. When you're knocked down, you jump back up as quickly as possible, and the difference between winning and losing is getting back up one more time than the other guy.

This can be difficult. You not only have to believe in yourself and whatever project you have undertaken to reach your goal, you also have to endure and defeat all the doubts about yourself that grow within you, and all the doubts that others may express about your chance of success.

That's painful. Not the pain of a broken arm or a migraine headache, but the emotional pain of questioning yourself and everything you have demanded of those around you, including family, friends and employees. How many times can you get back on your feet? How much pain can you really endure?

Nobody can answer that except you, of course. But I'm often reminded of a sign that hangs on the wall of the swimming camp my children attend:

Pain is temporary.
Glory is forever.

The cost of success, then, includes a good deal of sacrifice, and this is where another line is drawn between those who make it and those who don't.

It's relatively easy for a single person to sacrifice some of their social life to reach the goal they want, as I did in my twenties, when I would pass up a party to finish a business proposal or meet some customer's demands. There would always be another party, another chance to relax one way or another, but there might not be another chance to snare a big contract that would put us over the top of our quota for the month, or to score a hit with a key customer who would lead us to a number of other customers. It's what you do when building a business, and it's far easier when you're young and single than when you're mature with family obligations.

It also helps if you can get by with less sleep than other people. I require perhaps four hours of sleep a night. Getting more sleep isn't relaxing or rejuvenating to me, it's wasteful. We are all granted the same number of hours in a day, and one of the things that separates us is the way we use those hours. If you can't function with less than eight or nine hours of sleep every night, you may want to rethink plans of launching and running your own business.

Of course, the need for less sleep may be more related to an urge to succeed than to physical needs alone.

I'm not a stickler about punctuality at the office, except when a meeting is scheduled. Still, I'll wonder about someone who arrives later in the morning than expected, looking frazzled, and I may ask, "What kept you late?" If the answer mentions the terrible rush-hour traffic, I point out that there are no traffic jams at 5:30 in the morning.

If commuting to work represents a problem to an employee, I suggest they find a practical means of dealing with it, which usually means raising their level of commitment. Sitting in traffic and muttering about your commuting problems will not eliminate the problem. Increasing your commitment is the first step to take, and if arriving an hour or two earlier sounds too difficult, perhaps you should reassess your commitment.

You Don't Have to Think Like Me—But It Helps

Do I expect everyone who works for me to keep the same hours as I do? No, not everyone. Only those who choose, and are able, to keep up with me and duplicate some of the things I have achieved. I recognize that some see their job as a 9-to-5 obligation and are either not interested in reaching exceptional heights in their career or are unable to do so because of their personal situation.

Some are easily satisfied by reaching an acceptable level of success, a plateau where they can relax a little. I've seen employees start at a basic salary and apply their skills and energy at a ferocious level until they have reached a position justifying a six-figure salary—taking them from $30,000 to $100,000 annually—then they flatline. They deem their achievement good enough. Their goals were limited and, once met, the fire in their bellies cools down. This doesn't eliminate or reduce their value to me as an employee. But it limits their importance.

Advice from Joan Rivers

Comedienne Joan Rivers is over the top in some ways, and down to earth in others. While appearing on her television show *How'd You Get So Rich?* I grumbled a little about having to run off to do a television interview. "Honey," Joan said, "when they call and ask you to do something, go and do it because there will come a time when they don't call you at all."

I'm something of a reluctant celebrity, but Joan made me realize the importance of responding to invitations and opportunities when you're hot and wanted, because someday you'll be cold and unknown.

30

Never Start a Business You Can't Run Yourself

People who are not dentists should not launch dental practices. This might appear foolishly obvious, but I say it to prove a point about the errors made by short-sighted entrepreneurs, including many pitchers on *Dragons' Den*. I am constantly amazed at the number of people, for example, who know nothing at all about manufacturing and distribution, yet believe they can launch a company producing and distributing devices that require moulds and assembly. Their idea may be valid, but only when licensed to a company that understands the process.

Wise financial advisers employ a rule they insist their clients follow, especially clients saving for their retirement years without a lot of investment knowledge. The rule is: never put your money into an investment you do not understand. Starting a business you cannot run on your own is equally foolish.

Having said that, with my experience in the restaurant and movie business, what am I doing in computer services? Restaurants are labour intensive, but I learned a good deal working at Remys and St-Hubert. So why didn't I use that as a springboard to launch my own restaurant? And I saw the inner workings of TV studios and movie productions. Why didn't it spark an interest in *that* field, perhaps with a video production house or a cable channel?

It's not that I don't believe these are business opportunities. Restaurants, especially in Toronto, have a high turnover ratio, but I doubt if it's much higher than the failure rate of new ventures in other business sectors.

The reasons I remain in the computer service industry are because I understand it and, if necessary, I could assume almost all the duties involved in running the company on my own. I wouldn't be as innovative as the programming and technology teams in my business, or as effective in reaching prospects as the marketing experts, or perhaps even as victorious at racking up new business as our sales staff. But I could do all of these things well enough to save The Herjavec Group if it were necessary, and continue to do it until I found someone else to assume the chore.

The prospect of sinking my heart, soul and liquid assets into a company whose entire operation is in the hands of others, and is beyond my ability to rescue, scares the heck out of me. I don't understand lawyers, for example, who take the helm of a company whose business has no relation to the practice of law. The idea remains as strange to me as it would undoubtedly sound to them if I were to decide to practise law.

You may believe that someone who can't boil water could open a restaurant and operate it successfully, or someone who can't stand on skates could invest in a hockey camp. Not me. If I cannot take direct action to save both the company and my investment in it, I'm out. As you should be.

In the Beginning, Do Everything

From time to time, people talk to me about starting their own business. After describing their product or service, and perhaps their marketing and promotion plan, they'll discuss staffing. "First person I'll hire is a good accountant," they may offer, "and a really good sales rep to get out and beat the bushes for business."

If this is their first business venture, my usual response is: Don't hire anybody. Do everything yourself in the beginning.

It's not just a matter of minimizing your overhead costs in the first few months, although that's always an important factor. It's about learning as many aspects of your business as possible while things remain simple enough to do it. You don't need to be a chartered accountant to be a successful businessman, and you are not likely to need one on staff for the first several months. Even basic bookkeeping—writing your income in one column and your expenses in another—shouldn't be beyond your ability or your available time. When financial problems crop up, you'll be much better equipped to understand them if you've performed some of these chores yourself when just getting started.

And if the heart of your new business is your passion and vision, why would you conceal it from your customers, especially the ones you hope to snare in the first stages of your operation? That's why, in the beginning, your company should have no better salesperson than yourself. Among other things, you will never have to ask your sales staff to do something you haven't done, such as making cold calls, and the experience will enable you to understand the problems they may encounter.

Some entrepreneurs, when faced with a challenge they feel they can't handle themselves, rely on consultants. They assume that expertise not flowing through the veins of an owner can be transfused into the corporate veins of a struggling business—in exchange for substantial fees, of course.

If the consultants are so adept at suggesting how to run your business, why aren't they running one like it? Is consultancy that profitable? Or is it easier to tell someone how to be successful without actually following the directions yourself? I have seen many companies throw money at consultants, only to fail anyway. If you are unable to deal with a problem, hire a full-time employee who is capable of solving it perpetually, not a group of people from another city with wide smiles and large fees who vanish when the bills are paid (and remember who is paying the bills).

You can't do everything in your business forever. But during its earliest days, when things are simple and the structure is small, you not only should be able to do everything; you *must*.

Undercapitalization Can Be a Problem; Overcapitalization Can Be a Challenge

The most common reason for the failure of new business ventures is, supposedly, undercapitalization. Countering this assertion is the large number of ventures that grew from little or no capitalization into large, successful corporations. In many cases, the amount of drive and determination in the hearts of their founders proved more important than the amount of capital in the bank.

Having sufficient capitalization is fine. Having excess capitalization can lead to problems, including substantial losses and wasted time and energy.

The first two companies I worked for were capitalized by other people. The third company was my own. I launched it out of sheer necessity—I needed a job—and with about as much initial capital as you may have in your wallet right now. My current company, The Herjavec Group, was backed by millions of dollars. It also boasted the smartest, most experienced team of senior people of any of my companies, along with my own deep understanding of the business and extensive list of industry contacts.

Only one of those four companies lost money in its first year of operation. Care to guess which?

In the first eight months of operation, The Herjavec Group, composed of experienced and savvy managers, lost $650,000. By that point, most start-up companies would have been forced by their banks and investors to throw in the towel.

The Herjavec Group's biggest problem will probably make some entrepreneurs smirk in disbelief, but it's true: it had too much money.

Lack of money for families and individuals is no treat. I know this from my own childhood. Lack of money for a start-up company isn't much fun either, but it creates a discipline that forces clarity of thought. With no cash in the bank, you don't enjoy the luxury of casually choosing among a list of alternative strategies, or of waiting to discover whether some previous tactics will work if given more time. You get out and hustle because, if you don't, you starve.

Patience may be a virtue, but not in a cash-strapped start-up company. The money I put behind The Herjavec Group bought us time, but it didn't bring us customers, and never would have had we continued to wait for some new strategy to pay off.

Upon launching The Herjavec Group, I told myself that I could expect some short-term losses. Every new company does. I held back my impatience because I had enough cash that I didn't need to generate immediate profit. For the better part of our first year of operation I watched money flow out of the company and shrugged it off, believing something would turn up, some large contract would come our way to wipe out the loss.

But it didn't, not based on the way we were running things. Only when I told myself and my partners, "That's it—we're not losing another dime from this point on," did we find a formula that worked for us. We grew more aggressive in our business pitches and more focused on delivering customer value. In essence, we grew hungry and made the phones ring.

Obviously, cash is vital to companies actively fulfilling their contracts with clients and customers. And sufficient cash in the bank can help the owners of new companies sleep at night. But when you relax with too much cash in your account and no need to hustle for a buck every day, you risk extinguishing the fire in your belly that drove you to become an entrepreneur in the first place.

One of the amazing things about *Dragons' Den* is that pitchers are willing to give up such large chunks of their equity. It always makes me wonder why they started a business in the first place. As an entrepreneur, your only reward for all that sweat and toil is the equity—that's how an owner gets paid. You should hold on to it as long as possible. I've heard the old adage that it's better to own a small piece of a big company than a big piece of a small company. I'm not so sure. The odds of building something truly great, where 10 per cent of it will be worth a fortune, are very long.

I built my first business using credit cards and a mortgage on my house—and when I sold the company, I got to keep 100 per cent of the proceeds. I had a friend who started a business and ended up selling it for ten times what mine sold for; but he ended up pocketing a fraction of what I did. I have always believed that the ultimate payback for an owner is equity. Be careful what you give up, and for what reason.

31

Everything in Life Involves Selling Something

Some aspects of selling, and some people who make a living at it, give salesmanship a bad name. This doesn't diminish its importance in business or in life. As a young boy I watched my parents, who were struggling financially, deal with the actions of an unscrupulous door-to-door salesman. I hated what this man did to our family, both financially and emotionally.

It happened a year or two after we arrived in Canada from Croatia. I returned home from school one day, expecting the usual warm greeting from my mother and questions from my father about the things I had learned in class. This day was different.

I heard my father shouting in anger even before I opened our apartment door. My mother was in tears, repeating over and over again that she was sorry, but my father wouldn't stop berating her.

"What's wrong?" I asked my parents, demanding an answer, until Dad stopped insulting my mother long enough to thrust some sheets of paper at me.

"Look what she's done!" he shouted. "Look how stupid she's been!"

I had never heard Dad use this word to describe my mother. We both knew she was not stupid. What could she possibly have done?

I looked at the papers he handed me. They were a contract to purchase a vacuum cleaner. We didn't need a vacuum cleaner. It took three or four strokes of a broom to sweep the floor of any room in our tiny apartment. But some door-to-door shyster had convinced Mom to buy an expensive and elaborate vacuum cleaner system complete with more tools than you would need to clean the Taj Mahal, all for just a few dollars down. I looked at the terms. It was going to take years to pay off the debt.

"I'm sorry, I'm sorry," Mom kept saying through her tears.

"Send it back," I said to Dad. "This guy took advantage of us. We don't have to pay for this."

"It's a contract," Dad replied, reaching for his jacket. "Once you sign a contract, you live up to it. That's what you do in this country." And he stormed out the door. Mom sat crying while I slumped in a chair, trying to imagine how anybody could be as greedy as the vacuum cleaner salesman. He had taken advantage of my mother's poor command of English and of her desire to maintain a clean home for us, putting us in debt to make a few dollars for himself.

How Did He Do It? And Why?

We would always be outsiders, I realized. The only true leveller, the only thing that was certain to command respect for us, was money. Nothing was respected more than money in North American society. If that's what it took to be treated well, I would find a way to become so wealthy that no one would take advantage of me or my family again.

Pretty dramatic stuff for a twelve-year-old kid to think about, but it's a lesson I never forgot, and it shaped me from that day forward. I can't mark my compulsion to achieve success as a result of humiliation from that experience alone. Like so many things that change our view of the world, however, this one remained on my mind, like an emotional scar. Would a woman who spoke English from birth have been pushed into a deal like that? I suspected she wouldn't. And I suspected rich people wouldn't either, even if they could easily afford to buy the vacuum cleaner and all the toys that hung off it. Knowledgeable people would be confident enough to show the salesman the door. But people like my mother, desperate to fit into a different society, might be sold something they didn't need at a price they couldn't afford.

Nobody was sold things in the Croatian village where I grew up. They bought things they needed, but being convinced to spend thousands of dollars they couldn't afford on something they didn't need by someone they had never met before—why, that was unheard of. In fact, it was almost criminal.

How did the salesman do it? That's what I wondered. Despite my father's harsh words, my mother was a bright woman. She had difficulty with English, yes. But she knew what the word "no" meant. Why didn't she use it? And if she did, how did the salesman overcome it? Like the pious churchgoer who is intrigued by sin, I couldn't stop thinking about the salesman's technique.

I knew his motivation; it was clearly greed. And I had a good idea of his lack of morality; he recognized the purchase would be a financial hardship, but it didn't matter.

I long ago understood that you can be an outstanding business-person, admired by your employees and colleagues while assembling an impressive net worth, and be less than admirable in your own home. On a variation of that, you can also be a superb sales-person who achieves great success by applying your talents in an entirely immoral manner.

I am an admirer of anyone with great selling skills. I have equal disdain for those who discard their moral values in applying those same skills to meet a quota or score a commission.

Four Qualities of Outstanding Salespeople

1. **They believe in what they do.** Selling is difficult and demand-ing, especially when the economy is bad. Handling the inevitable rejection and failures is impossible without total commitment to your job as a salesperson.
2. **They enjoy and engage people.** Effective salespeople make buyers feel good about their decision, and they do this by engaging other people.
3. **They listen more than they talk.** By listening closely, good salespeople learn about needs and concerns, and know when and how to employ sales techniques.
4. **They eliminate reasons not to make the sale.** Positive atti-tudes are wonderful, but they alone are not enough to elimin-ate buyer objections. Countering buyer objections effectively is the single most important talent of a good salesperson.

32

Everyone in Your Organization Should Be a Salesperson

A poster first printed a generation ago can still be found hanging in a lot of sales managers' offices across the country. The illustration may vary, but the text is the same. It reads:

Nothing happens until somebody sells something.

Obviously, it's directed towards salespeople who head out the door or pick up the telephone each day to sell some company's product or service. But I believe it means more than that. I believe that, to one degree or another, our sales ability is related to our overall success in life. As Robin Williams said in *Cadillac Man,* the closest you can get to another person without sleeping with them is to sell them something. It really is that primal, that fundamental.

Selling isn't always about convincing the other person to hand over money in exchange for a product or service. Viewed in this, its crassest form, salesmanship is limited to people who sell overpriced used cars off a grimy lot, or the man who arrived at my parents' apartment door selling vacuum cleaners—a guy whose agenda was dedicated to his own needs, not my mother's or our family's. Good salespeople—the ones who maintain successful careers over several years—put the customer's needs ahead of their own, creating satisfaction for both sides.

Too many people, in my experience, refuse to acknowledge the role that selling plays in their lives, both the business and personal sides. If you were to gather a hundred employed people in a room and ask how many of them believe they perform a sales function each day, only a handful would raise their hands. The rest would shake their heads at the idea. In their view, they're technicians or managers or trainers; they're not salespeople.

Well, they're wrong. At its core, selling consists of relating to another person and persuading that person to go somewhere he or she perhaps had not planned to go. That's a very broad definition, I know, but if you reflect on it for a moment, it explains my claim that everything in life is about selling. We just call it something else.

A good physician or surgeon has to be successful at selling, especially when dealing with a patient who finds it difficult to accept the treatment they need to survive. Good lawyers need the same ability when persuading clients to agree to a strategy or settlement. And politicians need extraordinary sales ability to earn the trust of millions of voters.

Many of the things we do in the course of our lives are related to selling, but we give them different labels. Proposing to a future spouse or partner involves selling. In some cases we may call it seduction, but if you apply the definition I used earlier—persuading someone to go somewhere they hadn't planned on going—it's a sales process. Talking your children into changing their plans or their behaviour when needed involves sales techniques.

These kinds of actions come more easily to some people than to others. A few people appear to be born with natural sales abilities. The rest of us instinctively understand the basics to one degree or another. And everyone can learn techniques that sharpen their sales ability.

Since salesmanship becomes a factor in almost everything we do with our lives, we encounter lessons all around us, sometimes in the most surprising places. Like collection agencies, for example.

When Threats Don't Work, Salesmanship Does

I once worked the phones at a collection agency, calling people who were seriously in arrears in their bill payments. Collection agencies are the scrapyards of the business world. No matter how good or bad the economy may be, a certain percentage of every company's accounts receivable will be declared uncollectible through normal channels and handed to a collection agency.

Twenty years ago, collection agencies operated in a kind of Wild West environment compared with the restrictions placed on them today. Back then, you were permitted to call any time of the day or night and make almost any kind of threat or promise in order to recover the debt. The only criterion was, did you get money out of the deadbeat? If you succeeded at this single goal, all was forgiven.

Working the phones at a collection agency is as tough a business as you could ever encounter. You are pressured to use any
means necessary when dealing with the person on the other end
of the line, and the calls frequently end in shouting matches or
tears—the tears, of course, being shed by the individual who owes
the money, breaking down under threats.

At the end of my first day on the job, I discussed the experience
with my dad, who asked how things went. "Terrible," I replied. "I
hate it. I'm going back tomorrow to tell them I'm quitting."

"Ah," my dad said, "you can't finish anything," and he dismissed
me with a wave of his hand.

He couldn't have given me a bigger incentive to keep trying,
and I did. This time, instead of focusing on the drawbacks of the
job, I began looking into its mechanics, searching for ways to
make it more palatable to me and more successful for the company. I believed the solution could be found not in screaming but
in selling. I understood the basics of good sales technique, and I
looked for ways to apply them.

I learned that collection agencies are successful at recovering a
ridiculously low percentage of debts, as low as ten per cent. I also
learned that about twenty per cent of the people we called were
never going to pay, no matter how much I threatened or pleaded
with them.

Good salespeople know where to apply their energy with a
potential customer, and when to stop wasting their time on tire
kickers and window shoppers. Within two or three telephone calls
to the same individual, I was able to determine whether he or she
fell into the no-pay no-way twenty per cent, or could be persuaded

to cover their debts. I followed a policy of discarding the first group and concentrating on the second.

Roughly one in five people on my list, I determined, would pay up if they felt they were getting a good deal. This opened up opportunities for me. If I could collect half of the amount *they* owed, I'd be doing better than average on my collections, and they'd feel good enough about the deal to actually send the cheques they promised.

The key was to identify their style, their values and their expectations, using the same relationship-building methods employed by salespeople all over the world. For example, I might ask the debtor—let's call him Frank—whether he had gone to university. If he had, I'd follow up by asking if he was working in a field related to his studies. I would do this because, in my book, people who drop out of a university course because they find the work too hard, or who abandon a career path that normally offers job opportunities galore, want an easy path through life. They want to feel important and superior in some way, and one way is to believe they got the better side of a bargain. Which made them ideal candidates for my "Let's Make a Deal" technique.

Let's say Frank owed eight hundred dollars. I might tell him, "I'm not authorized to do this, but if you can get me, say, three hundred and fifty dollars today, I can get my boss to settle for that. Don't hold me to this, now. But get me the three-fifty today and I won't be calling you back."

It didn't matter to me if Frank bragged to his wife or buddies about the great deal he'd swung with the pushy collections guy, because I was collecting more than four times the amount that the agency expected to get. Plus, I never promised the balance would be forgiven.

I used other methods as well, all based not on standard collections agency process—which assumed the person on the other end would respond only to shouted threats over the phone—but on traditional sales methods: create a relationship with the customers, assess their interests and values, and offer something that met both their budget and their expectations.

After six months on the job, I had set a record for the volume of money collected by anyone at the agency's offices all across Canada. And that's when I quit. I had proven something to my father and to myself.

On the Way to "Yes!"

The method of choosing where and with whom to invest my time and effort on calls at the collections agency made an impact on the way I manage today, especially when it comes to sales.

Planning a sales pitch to a customer with my team begins by reviewing all the good things that are likely to happen, including reasons why the prospect will surely respond positively. "We've got the best product and the best price," one sales team member might boast. Another might add, "The engineers all love our product," and somebody else may suggest that a friend of her brother-in-law happened to know somebody in the prospect's head office who claimed that our pitch would be a sure thing, that we couldn't lose.

This is all very good at building team morale, I suppose, but my response at hearing it is to say, "Now tell me the reasons why we *won't* get the sale."

I'm not trying to be a wet blanket during these sessions. I'm trying to determine whether we are making the most effective use of our time and energy, and discover how we can ensure it will be as successful as everyone believes it will be. I'm looking for the no's that may be lurking among all those enthusiastic yes's.

One more time: you learn more from your failures than from your successes. This hardly means you should spend time unduly on projects that are unlikely to bring victory. Failure should be an unfortunate encounter, not a chosen experience, and experience, after all, is what you get when you are expecting something else.

So I ask everyone involved to tell me why the project will fail. Sometimes an element we hadn't addressed or some aspect of the deal that we can't influence appears insurmountable. When that happens, why bother? The potential customer may be the equivalent of the tire kickers and window shoppers I avoided at the collection agency, and I choose not to waste time on them.

The second reason for asking why we may not succeed is actually a means of ensuring that we *do* succeed.

In sales, every prospect has various reasons to say no. It may be price, it may be performance, it may be timing, it may be a dozen other things that we have control over. If we can identify them, we can usually find a way to eliminate them. And once we eliminate all the reasons for a prospect to say no, the only answer that remains is yes!

33

Have Fun

Good salespeople love the challenge of preparing a sales presentation. They review the customer's situation, assess the needs, match their product or service to the needs, find a way of emphasizing the value and ask for the order.

That's the standard textbook approach. But if you're truly driven to win, you'll add something else to the blend: fun.

We recently made a presentation to a large company involved in sophisticated technical work related to atomic energy. That's pretty serious stuff, and there was much to talk about and discuss with them. We did, but only among other subjects that generated a lot of laughter on both sides. At the end of the meeting the chief information officer shook my hand and said, "Wow, I didn't know technical information meetings could be so much fun!"

As we left the customer's building, I asked our salesperson what the customer would remember about the meeting.

"Our technical list," he answered, "and all the case studies we showed him about our experience working on—"

I stopped him right there. "He's not going to remember any of that stuff," I said. "What he'll remember about this meeting is that it was fun. He'll get all the technical data he needs when he needs it. For now, he'll associate us with competence, and remember the fun he had. And that's what will bring us his business."

This example acknowledges a special characteristic of the human memory process. Looking back over our lives, we remember major events that happened and recall our feelings clearly, but we rarely remember the words that were spoken at the time with similar accuracy. The same process applies to a business meeting. Was it productive? Sure was! Was it enjoyable? It was actually fun! Was the time productively spent? Definitely! So, what were the exact words spoken by everyone at the meeting?

No one remembers, of course. It's the feelings, both positive and negative, that burn their way into our memory.

Educators long ago realized that the best environment for children to learn in was one in which they had fun playing at some activity related to their lesson. Acting out the Norman invasion of Britain in 1066, either with toy soldiers or by performing on a stage, is not only more fun to a ten-year-old child, it makes a greater impact. We should all remember that somewhere within our psyche is the ten-year-old kid we all used to be, and he or she still influences our life, including the part of our mind involved in making business decisions.

Watch for Telling Details

The last thing you want to leave your prospects feeling is confused. Leaving them feeling good is a giant step towards closing a sale.

Here's another example about making a customer feel good.

We were making a pitch to a firm in Montreal and getting nowhere. The product and price were right; based on the benefits we could deliver, we should have long since clinched the sale.

"What's the problem?" I asked the representative calling on the Montreal customer.

"The problem is the procurement guy," he replied. "He's a hard-ass. Tough as nails and really negative. I just can't get through to him."

"Set up another meeting with him," I said. "This time, I'll come with you."

A few weeks later, both of us arrived at the prospective customer's office, where we were greeted formally by a man in his mid-fifties wearing a well-tailored suit, starched shirt and perfectly knotted tie. While my sales guy began opening his books and nervously preparing his presentation, I took a closer look at the procurement officer and noticed he was wearing Chanel eyeglasses. Now, that was telling. What kind of formal hard-ass guy wears Chanel glasses?

Maybe he's not the guy my salesperson decided he is, I speculated. Maybe he's a guy who enjoys designer accessories just for the fun of wearing them. Maybe he's hipper than we realize.

Before my salesperson could launch his presentation, I waved him off and began asking the prospect about his background with the company, leading into whatever personal comments the prospective customer wanted to discuss. None of our conversation involved the technical material we'd brought with us. The entire meeting was spent learning about the procurement officer's background, personal interests, work history with the corporation and other topics that many people may class as trivial, but which I knew were important to him. Then we shook hands and left.

Later, we reviewed the session. "You're still new at this game," I told the salesman. "You don't have enough experience to do two different things at the same time and do both of them well. You had your promotional material and the quote in front of you, with your pen in your hand. You were all set to grab an order, but you weren't ready yet to do this and still concentrate on the customer."

I explained that I would rather see the salesman look at the customer—and not his sales material—when he first arrived, then find something to talk about that interested the customer. When the customer asks, "Where's the quote?" you follow his lead and hand it across the desk. Instead of doing two or three things passably well, I wanted my salesman to do one thing exceptionally well, which was to reach the personal side of the customer, not the business side. Within a few days of that presentation, we locked up the sale. We had a major new customer on our client list. And all because I noticed the logo on his glasses.

People at big companies will nod when they read this and mutter, "Nothing new here, selling is always about building relationships." Well, yes, it is. But seasoned salespeople may have had years to build that relationship, and to some degree the clients and customers already had a "relationship" with a company knowing who they were, what they did and how well they did it. Smaller companies—especially smaller and newer companies— don't enjoy that benefit.

There's no magic in building a great customer relationship over several years. There is definitely magic in doing it within a couple of months, or after a couple of meetings. People in traditional companies say it can't be done. I say it can, because my staff and I have done it. In our business, where the products, service requirements and applications change frequently and much of the industry reinvents itself in a matter of months, creating strong rapport and loyalty among customers is essential. On that basis, being able to adapt to changing customers and their expectations represents an important skill for salespeople. Good salespeople function as chameleons, adapting to their surroundings as needed, usually without even thinking about it.

As the lesson of the man in the designer eyeglasses proved, you need to almost instantly size up your customer and choose your strategy. It's not a matter of stereotyping, but a matter of searching for clues. In our business, it determines the selling strategy we will use. In the retail industry, it identifies just how much time and effort you choose to invest in the customer.

34

Look Good

We've all encountered salespeople who recite us data about a product as though they're reading from a brochure or a promotion manual, feeding the same feature list to every customer. They may think they're selling, but they're not. The very best salespeople are versatile. They can assess a potential buyer and environment and instinctively adapt their sales pitch accordingly, establishing the necessary relationship almost immediately. They are also enthusiastic about the product or service they are selling. You cannot sell something you do not believe in—not effectively, anyway. You cannot sell something whose benefits you don't fully appreciate, either. I learned these rules during a short-lived but productive career on the sales floor at Harry Rosen, the country's leading upscale menswear chain.

When it seemed as though the video and movie industry could perhaps show me the way to success, I thought I might as well dress for it. While I waited for it to happen, I visited Harry Rosen's flagship store to purchase a made-to-measure suit. I don't know how much I expected to pay, but it wasn't nearly as much as I discovered it would cost me. Fifteen hundred dollars for a jacket and pair of pants? Yikes! I couldn't afford to shop there. But when I learned that Harry Rosen sales staff were entitled to purchase a new suit at a 70–per-cent discount every six months, I decided I could afford to *work* there.

So I became a menswear salesman for a time, helping others choose the suits, shirts, ties and accessories that would deliver the look of success, which most of them had already achieved. The job expanded my wardrobe, improved my taste in fashion and provided me with new insight into what makes a great salesperson, and why some sales staff should find themselves a new career. Each Saturday morning, Harry or a sales trainer would arrive at the store and review items from the current merchandise mix or promotional campaign, explaining the customer benefits and how the sales staff could use them to make a sale. I never failed to pick up something of value from these sessions that I could use when dealing with customers, yet about half the sales staff chose not to attend the meetings, which totally confused me. Did they know all the features of the new fashions, or all the sales techniques to use on the floor?

Rosen himself was a dominant presence, with an aura that was reinforced (as you might expect) by the way he was dressed. I didn't want to launch my career in retail menswear, but I definitely wanted to learn how to recreate his presence.

The retail experience underlined what I already knew about selling from instinct, especially the importance of creating a relationship with the customer. The first step involved applying a quick qualification process to prospective customers. I needed to know whether the man entering the door could afford the expensive items on display or was merely window shopping on the inside. Without drawing final conclusions, I learned to divide browsers into the "Has the Money" group and the "Just Looking" crowd with two quick glances, and (if you'll forgive the pun) tailor my approach accordingly.

If you're a man, try this for yourself the next time you enter a high-end menswear store. When a salesperson approaches you, note how he or she quickly and subtly looks at two items: your shoes and your watch. Stroll in wearing Florsheims and a Rolex, and you can expect the salesperson to hang on every word you utter. Slip an old pair of sneakers on your feet and a Timex on your wrist, and you're likely to hear little more than "Have a nice day..."

Dress for Success

- **Clothes don't make the man or woman, but they do make an impression.**
- **You don't have to be good-looking to create a powerful presence, or tall to be imposing, or young to appear vibrant.** But you do need to be well-dressed.
- **First impressions are subconscious but significant.** Dressing in a disorganized fashion communicates a similar impression—whether true or not—about your approach to business.
- **Dressing and grooming well is a summation of how you present yourself to the world.** Unless your appearance represents who you are, people will not know who (or what) "the real you" is, and that's regrettable.
- **Nobody wants to look like a bum.** Really.

35

Follow the Three Commandments

I've always tried to establish and follow various rules within the companies I launched. I aim to have ten rules for each situation, although I settle for fewer if necessary. A few rules change from time to time, depending on economic and competitive situations, product and pricing developments, and other factors. When it comes to the sales aspect of business, three rules have been consistent over the years, and they're worth presenting here.

The most fascinating thing about these rules, which I insist must be adhered to by every employee, is how effective they are in every aspect of life beyond business applications. Perhaps that's what makes them so important, and why they should be considered inflexible.

Rule #1: The stuff's gotta work. More than that, it has to perform up to specified levels.

No amount of sophisticated marketing expertise and polished sales techniques will save a situation if the product design, the technology behind it, or the vendor's service level fail to meet their promise. This should be a given in every business situation. Unfortunately, it's often missing.

Imagine shopping for a new car. When you enter the dealership, the salesperson greets you like a long-lost buddy and, in fact, it turns out that she's related to a distant cousin of yours. You're served coffee and snacks on expensive bone china, you're shown the model of car you want in exactly the colour you prefer, the price is within your budget and the dealer arranges for you to drive your shiny new car home that very night. This is a great buying experience.

The next morning, your new car doesn't start. The problem is traced to a faulty part that will have to be specially ordered. It could take weeks for the part to arrive and repairs to be made. Where is your wonderful sales experience now?

In my companies, if we are not 100-per-cent convinced that the installations we're selling to customers will perform up to specifications from the day the delivery is complete, we won't bother trying to sell it. That's not an attempt to achieve some kind of high righteousness. It's just good business practice.

Rule #2: It's not what you say; it's how you make people feel.

I dealt with this earlier, but it bears repeating because it's so important, yet so easily overlooked.

To some people, the idea of having fun in a business session sounds like heresy. To them, the word "business" is preceded by the word "serious," which suggests that they are caught up in their own sense of importance. Yet, amid all the statistics, charts, graphs, cost-benefit figures and general content of a sales presentation, prospects remain involved in dealing with various personal crises and decisions. They appreciate any salesperson who can simplify at least one facet of their lives, and a stack of statistics or a library of charts rarely accomplishes this on its own. An element of true rapport, no matter how brief or how motivated, will always be appreciated and rarely forgotten.

The day following a presentation, almost no one who attended the event from the potential buyer's side will recall all the details with clarity. But every one of them, I can assure you, will remember how they felt during and after the event—bored, elated, disappointed, inspired, relieved, concerned. Pick the positive feelings out of that list and strive to create them in your audience when making a sales presentation.

Rule #3: The first five minutes dictate everything that happens afterward.

This echoes the idea that the margin of the sale begins as soon as you walk through the door. It's more than a matter of making good first impressions. In some cases, it shapes the impact of your entire presentation.

The first impression is made within the first minute. From that point, you have four minutes to either correct a bad initial impression or strengthen a positive one. Everything else that happens through the rest of the presentation substantiates the way the audience felt during those first five minutes.

Like a lot of truths we encounter in life, some of this may sound obvious in the beginning. But to many salespeople it's not. Until you recognize how and why these rules apply, you won't be conscious of using them when necessary, and if you fail to use them you're not achieving your full potential.

So here's a test: forget about those three rules in a business context. Think of them in the context your own life, including meeting and choosing a spouse (*the first five minutes* . . .); helping your children deal with problems (*it's not what you say, it's how you make them feel* . . .); and negotiating a job situation, perhaps seeking a salary raise with your boss (*the stuff's gotta work* . . .).

As I said earlier, everything in life is about sales.

36

The Best People Don't Always Apply for the Job

Effective managers never fail to acknowledge that their business success is based primarily on the ability to select and motivate their support staff. Which means that one of the most valuable management skills you can have is the ability to recognize and choose the talent you need, whenever and wherever it appears.

Consider the traditional methods of hiring outstanding employees in critical job functions. You can rely on a headhunter to find the talent you need, and pay a hefty service fee. You can hope that the best members of your current staff mature until they're ready to assume greater responsibilities just when you need them to step up. Or you can launch a long parade of hopefuls whenever an opening appears, choosing the best from among whatever group happens to appear.

But here's a fourth approach: you can develop, and rely on, the ability to spot exceptional talent that you know will be an asset to your business, and find a role for them.

I was fortunate enough to encounter and hire two men who played critical roles in helping me achieve success with my firm in just that manner. In fact, their business talents and personal qualities were so impressive that I recruited them years later as cofounders of my current company, The Herjavec Group. The latter choice, besides being less expensive, is often more rewarding when it comes to uncovering exceptional abilities and building enduring relationships.

"I Won't Take Your Card, but I'll Give You a Job"

One day, I answered the telephone to hear a man making a pitch for a credit card. It was a classic telemarketing proposition back in the days when they were less restricted, and my first instinct was to say no and hang up. But I noticed something unique in this person's delivery. The words, I suspected, were scripted, but the caller was inserting a lot of persuasion into the message, enough for me to stay on the line and assess his salesmanship, even though I wasn't in the market for the product he was selling. When I asked hard questions about the deal, his answers were convincing. And when I raised objections, he dissolved them with his smooth, convincing responses.

Finally, I said, "Look, I'm not interested in a credit card, but you're a darn good salesman. How much are they paying you to do this?"

"I can't tell you that," the man replied.

"Why don't you come by tomorrow and talk about working for me?" I said. I was turning the telemarketing process around, making a serious offer to someone out of the blue who had called me at random. To some surprise on my part, he agreed, and the next day George Frempong walked into my office.

It quickly became clear that George, while a terrific natural salesman, knew nothing about computers. But, I reminded myself, neither did I when I started. Besides, I was immediately impressed by his drive to succeed and his ability to communicate. He was confident without being arrogant, direct without being brash, ambitious without being heartless. This, I recognized, was a diamond in the rough.

So I handed him a script and a list of potential clients. "We're launching a seminar," I explained, "and if you use this script, applying your personal sales abilities when talking to these prospects, you'll fill the seminar room for me. And if you do, you're going to have a terrific job here."

That was almost fifteen years ago as I write this. George rose to become an executive in my company and others, and was a cofounder of The Herjavec Group. And he's still a heck of a salesman.

Sharing a Vision with a Brilliant Guy

My critical first sale to a customer did more than get my company started. It also introduced me to the guy who became the chief technology officer with my first firm, and who now holds the same position with The Herjavec Group.

When it comes to technical issues involving computers and Internet security, Sean Higgins is simply the smartest guy I've ever met. Having earned a master's degree in electrical engineering and applied physics, Sean was employed in the U.S. office of my first customer, and he came to Canada to oversee the installation. We hit it off, I described my vision of the company and its future, and somewhere along the way I offered him a job. He accepted, and his technological expertise immediately propelled us to a new level of customer service.

Sean has played a key role in designing and implementing our network and security strategies, and he can match anyone in theory and execution of technical challenges where computer security is concerned.

Sean and the team he built over the years have done more than generate the service quality that made us successful; they improved my own achievements as the prime salesman for the company. The more you believe in the product and service you're selling, and the more convinced you are that the competition cannot compare in value and performance with the item you want the customer to buy, the better you are at selling it.

I believe Sean can do anything technically associated with the services my sales staff and I promote. Whenever we make a pitch to potential customers, we can—and do—promise to meet their needs completely because we have total confidence in Sean's abilities. He never lets us down. More important, he has never let the customer down.

Between George Frempong's innate sales ability and Sean Higgins's technical ingenuity, we had a one-two punch that enabled me to focus on broader issues, especially when it came to making major management decisions. Which can be a challenge for people like me who are more attuned to dealing with short-term crises than long-term cruising. Naturally, George and Sean were the first two people I approached when I formed The Herjavec Group, and both are cofounders of the company.

My instincts and strategies regarding the company and the talents of George and Sean have been proven correct. The Herjavec Group, as I write this, is the country's largest supplier of Internet security systems and software.

37

Humility Is More Effective than Arrogance

It's never pleasant when things go wrong, but it's never wise to assume the other person is to blame either. When things do go wrong, however, it's a good time to learn how to improve the way you do business, and to appreciate the difference between optimism and realism.

The longer I'm in business, the more I realize that success almost never hinges exclusively on the quality of your product or service. It also involves, to a larger extent than you may realize, the people you deal with and the way they relate to each other.

You need talent, dedication, qualifications and all the usual textbook-described skills among the key people on your team. I've learned over the years to look for something else, however: the intangible ability to create a personal bond with customers and clients. Some of this talent can be learned, and a good deal of it is a natural offshoot of everyone's personality, but most is acquired by understanding the things that make others react in a positive manner.

We all hide our inner selves to some extent. Role-playing—usually as a defensive manoeuvre—is common among business-people who don't know each other well. The salesperson who can identify the real person behind the role the prospect is playing, and know how to respond to his or her values, has an enormous advantage.

I tend to read people's natures and personalities with success. Perhaps I picked up this ability as a little boy wandering through my village, watching and listening to grown-ups, or maybe as the immigrant who desperately wanted to understand how this new society he found himself in actually worked. I don't know, and I don't really care. I know I honed the skill over the years until it became an important part of my running my businesses, and I have tried to pass the lesson along to people in my companies.

You've heard a variation from me on this already: **a successful sale depends not as much on how well you communicate the content of your pitch as how good you make people feel.** You won't find this rule in traditional sales manuals, which are more focused on identifying features and benefits, handling objections and knowing when and how to close. Yet I have watched salespeople follow all the tried and proven techniques of supposedly successful selling and still walk away without an order. Why? **Because they failed to make the customer feel good about it.**

I'm not talking only about a decision to buy a new sofa or car. The same principle applies to making multi-million-dollar purchasing decisions for large corporations as it does when shopping for furniture. No matter how big and powerful your customer may be, you cannot ignore the fact that the most important subject for people to discuss is themselves. Most people feel good about doing this, and the memory of the feeling they get remains long after details about the features and benefits covered in your sales pitch have grown fuzzy. You don't create this feeling over an hour-long meeting. You have only the first five minutes to do the job. The rest of the meeting substantiates and reinforces the initial impression.

So, what do you want the customer to recall about the meeting? If you're successful, it won't be details on the technical specifications or the service agreement. It will be the way the customer felt when the meeting ended.

Where Did We Go Wrong? It Pays to Find Out

Nothing works perfectly, including even my theory about having fun in meetings and establishing immediate rapport with the customer. You can work hard to achieve these goals and still fail to win the business. So it's important to know how to react when the results are not what you anticipated (and we all anticipate success, of course).

Although each is admittedly set in a dramatic and somewhat artificial environment, *Dragons' Den* represents this scenario in a microcosm. The pitchers arrive prepared to score a victory, and they encounter scepticism, derision and outright rejection from at least some of the Dragons.

Many respond with anger, and some with tears. These reactions make for great television viewing, but they never succeed in changing anything. But from time to time, we encounter pitchers who not only handle the rejection gracefully, they later find the best way—in fact, the only effective way—of countering the rebuff: they succeed despite the negative response.

Perhaps the most heartening example was the appearance on *Dragons' Den* of two young women from Saskatchewan who sought funding for their costume jewellery company. Four of us, including me, chose not to do a deal. I liked their concept, their skill and their determination, but I was too concerned about the amount of time it might take to establish the brand. Kevin O'Leary's rejection was typically bellicose. Questioning the young women's sales projections and valuations, he asked them from the elevated stage: "Do you take drugs? Yes or no." He went further, calling their venture "a drug deal," claiming there was no chance for the company to make money. He concluded his rejection with, "This should be called I'm Really Small Cockroach Jewellery Incorporated."

I cannot imagine anything like a similar reaction from serious businesspeople. The women kept their dignity in the face of Kevin's onslaught. Brett Wilson chose to participate, which proved a wise move. The company, at last report, is exceeding its original sales projections.

I cringe when I recall Kevin's caustic comments to two young women who were simply pursuing the same kind of dream that the Dragons supposedly support in principle, and while I have never experienced anything nearly as bitter as Kevin's observations from my clients, I'm familiar with the emotions that rejection, especially the incomprehensible kind, can generate. I have also learned the best way of handling it.

Soon after my first company was on its feet, we made a pitch to a substantially sized firm whose operation demanded a complex and fail-proof solution. We spent weeks putting everything in place. We isolated the prospect's primary need, tailored the benefits to meet it, calculated the cost savings, created a complete service program and tied everything up in a package that, in our opinion, could not be surpassed by our competition. It was the very best deal the customer could have received. This wasn't just speculation; we had determined that nobody could match the benefits we were offering this company at our price.

On the day of the presentation, we established a good rapport with everyone present. From the beginning, the meeting appeared to go well. We returned to our office confident that we had scored a major win, only to learn that they had awarded the contract to a larger company than ours for the contract.

Before we chalked this one up to experience, I wanted to go a few more steps with the prospect. We had gone into the presentation with confidence that bordered on arrogance, and now I suggested it was time to exhibit a little humility. I wanted to know what we had done wrong and correct it in future pitches. I also wanted to lay the groundwork for a second pitch to this client— one we would be certain to win.

The top man at the company refused to accept my telephone call, assuming, I suppose, that I would either complain about mistreatment or beg for another chance. I wanted to do neither, of course. I managed to reach a member of the CEO's staff who agreed to talk with me. After introducing myself, I mentioned that we had spent weeks assembling the presentation to his firm and we were very disappointed about not winning the business. "We respect your decision, of course," I added quickly, "based upon your greater knowledge of your business and your needs. I just wondered if we could take a few minutes while you explained to me how we could have done a better job."

My belief that we had the obviously superior deal for this prospect had been so strong that it may have generated arrogance on our part, although I prefer to call it overconfidence. That kind of self-assurance is neither unusual nor necessarily bad in our business. Every successful salesperson I have encountered believed in the obvious superiority of whatever they were selling, leading to astonishment whenever a prospect failed to agree with him or her.

Replacing arrogance with humility worked. The customer staff member and I agreed to meet for coffee. He explained what had worked in our presentation and what hadn't, and I earned his assurance that we would be invited to pitch for the next contract. We were, and we won, and his company eventually grew into one of our largest customers.

Cut to the Chase

Entrepreneurs clearly have different skills from those of dedicated managers, and putting out fires that other people have started is not a primary talent for most of us. Still, there are times when problems demand attention and, while every problem deserves its own unique solution, it's possible to follow some general guidelines in dealing with them.

I prefer not to micromanage my company, but from time to time it's necessary. When I feel the need to tackle a problem and work my way through it from the inside out, I reduce the number of filters I'll encounter. Every employee between the problem and me represents a filter. Some are active, others are passive, but all influence my view of the situation. It's especially critical to eliminate filters when the problem involves customer satisfaction.

A manager or sales rep's normal response to my enquiries about a customer-based problem is usually to provide me with details of the situation. But I don't want to hear the details from my manager. I want to hear them from the source, before they've been filtered by the manager's self-protective instincts. This, of course, may displease the manager. It doesn't matter because, among other effects, it tends to reassure the customer. Everything in business begins and ends with your customer, and there is little to be gained by dividing your loyalty between your customer and your staff. Start with the customer, because the farther you are from the source of an event, the more diluted will be the facts you are fed.

How I Handle Customer Complaints

My years as a waiter gave me a solid grounding in dealing with customer complaints.

Handling multi-million-dollar deals calls for a more complex approach than handling an order of barbecued chicken dinners, but these always seem to apply.

- **Assume the client is right 99.9 per cent of the time.** Don't fight the fact. Accept it and move on.
- **Remember the role that customers play.** You are in business to serve your clients, who pay the bills and put food on your table.

- **How you fix things with clients is as important as what you fix.** Grumbling about the time and expense it may be costing you is counter-productive.
- **There is no such thing as a small complaint.** Every complaint represents a failure, and every failure must be addressed.
- **The ultimate complaints are usually expressed silently.** Clients may choose not to complain for various reasons and simply walk away, representing lost business.
- **The first response to a complaint must be good communication.** Ignore any complaint at your peril.
- **Test your system to anticipate and eliminate complaints.** If your business involves technology, don't use customer experiences to locate weaknesses. Keep testing your product to locate problems before your customers can.
- **Treat your employees like clients.** People who feel good about their product, their service and their employer take better care of their customers.
- **Solutions are important.** Blame is useless. There should be no time for finger-pointing on either side.
- **When the problem is solved, analyze.** The intention is not to assign blame. The goal is to find ways of preventing a reoccurrence.

38

Know What You Need to Know

We've all heard tales about companies whose sales are spectacular, whose brand is renowned, whose products are well-respected, and yet the company goes broke or at least falls into some kind of financial abyss. This occurs frequently in smaller companies whose founder and CEO takes a hands-on approach to the business. They often know everything necessary about their product, market and sales force, and not nearly enough about their company's financial situation.

I taught myself how to create and read balance sheets and profit-and-loss statements and understand what they are telling me. This enabled me to spot a problem before it threatened the company's stability. You don't need to become a good accountant to succeed in business (although you *do* need a good accountant to review your progress on a regular basis); you simply must know what you *need* to know. I can't tell you my company's debt-to-equity ratio or calculate various financial ratios at any given time. They're not relevant to me, and I can have somebody tell me that stuff when I need it. But I know when my cash flow is in trouble, when corporate expenses are eating up profits and when the sales curve is heading in the wrong direction.

When it comes to the financial side of things, you need to know where the safety measures are and how to apply them. Learning how to write and read balance sheets and P&L statements, and how to monitor cash flow from the first week of your company's existence, may divert time and effort from your business initially, but it's essential to your success. Don't leave such basic responsibility up to others.

The best analogy for this aspect of business success is to suggest that you are a physician and the business is your patient. You don't need to know what the patient eats every day or how much exercise he or she gets. But you certainly need to know the patient's general health and, when it declines, how to spot the disease and find the cure.

Sign All Your Own Cheques

I doubt that anyone in history has provided more advice on life than Oprah Winfrey. And it's clear that few people have built a fortune that even begins to compare with hers, thanks to the tens of millions of fans who hang on her every word.

I was fortunate to have Oprah as a neighbour on the island off the coast of Florida where we both have our winter getaway homes, and was pleased to meet her a few times. It was Oprah who provided one of the simplest, yet most effective, suggestions for business operators: always sign your own cheques. It worked for her, so I figured it would work for me. And it has.

Many people are surprised when I say this, usually asking: "How will you sign all your own cheques when your firm is doing $100 million, $200 million or more in business every year?" My response is that the ones I don't sign will get bigger.

With every company I have launched, in the beginning, no expense was paid unless it had my approval. Need forty-seven dollars for the postage meter? Get Robert to approve it. That was the rule. As the companies grew, I assigned others to handle smaller purchases, but insisted that larger expenditures not be paid without my signature on the cheque. The amount requiring my signature rises with the company's financial growth, but the principle always applies.

This is not a matter of trust. It's a matter of knowing and acknowledging how much money is flowing out of the company. If you're not aware of this factor in your firm, you might as well drive home blindfolded every night. Signing a cheque is your last chance to make sure everything is working as it should. If it isn't, don't sign the cheque. I have always found it easier to negotiate with a supplier or contractor before I've paid them than afterwards!

Being "Nice" Doesn't Mean Being Foolish

Such practices may lead to being labelled "tight-fisted" by some employees. If this bothers you, don't let it. You're in business to be successful, not to be loved. I'm not sure that the old adage "Nice guys finish last" is always valid, but to be honest, I would prefer to be known as successful and wealthy than "nice."

Even when his comments are unapologetically offensive, Kevin O'Leary, my fellow panellist on *Dragons' Den,* considers himself a nice guy. He's not being ironic. When he encounters someone whose business proposal is foolish and whose plans are unrealistic, Kevin sincerely believes he is doing the pitcher a good deed by pointing out the facts in the most direct and effective manner possible. Even a hint of encouragement in those situations, Kevin explains, is not doing the entrepreneur any favours. Just the opposite, in fact. He believes brutal honesty in these situations is essential, and delivering it is his obligation.

Kevin and I are clearly different in countless ways, but we share at least one quality that I expect most readers of this book would understand. We both want to be considered fair and pleasant to deal with. Whatever our gender, we all want to be "nice guys." But how "nice" can you be when running a business? I discovered the answer after paying the price.

An old acquaintance of mine was running a company that needed our services, and we submitted a proposal to deliver the security his firm needed. It wasn't the largest contract we chased that year, but it wasn't peanuts either, and when my friend agreed to the deal we completed the installation and sent the company an invoice.

Based on our friendship, I ignored my usual procedure of performing a complete credit check on the company before approving the deal. I discovered, despite my friend's assurances, that his firm was sliding towards insolvency. I had thought it would be an insult to assume my friend was telling me anything but the truth—nice guys don't doubt their friends, do they? Well, there was nothing "nice" about writing off that particular invoice.

It's important to make a distinction between cash and friends, even if it suggests you are not as "nice" as you may want the world to consider you. Friends are friends. Cash is cash. There is no reason to link them. Cash is also the lifeblood of a business. Like the blood that runs through your own veins and arteries, cutting off cash or significantly reducing its flow could be fatal to your business. Risking this eventuality is where being "a nice guy (or gal)" must end.

Friends still need help from time to time, and if you accumulate sufficient wealth a friend will almost certainly turn to you for assistance in the form of a loan. If and when this happens, you have one of two choices to make. You can say no, or you can hand over the money and explain that you do not expect to be paid back.

Under no circumstances should you lend your friend money. If you do, chances are you will lose both the cash and the friendship. It's best to preserve at least one.

Sometimes the most critical decisions I make in favour of the company create the risk of destroying the "nice guy" persona I prefer. When this occurs, how long do I pause before going ahead? Maybe half a heartbeat.

That's how long I took to consider a pitch made to me by a young woman selling a new device that promised added benefits for our Internet security programs. She brought it to The Herjavec Group before anyone else in recognition of our leadership position within the industry. I liked the product's operation, I liked its function and I liked its price. I liked everything about it except one thing.

"Who else will you be offering this to?" I asked.

Everyone else, she told me.

"There is no way we'll buy it today if you are selling it to our competitors next week," I replied. "We'll take it if we have exclusive use of it for a fixed period. If you want a sale, you've got it. But only under those conditions."

This was not what she expected. She believed, and I suspect she was correct, that signing our company would create leverage with other firms wanting to climb aboard the bandwagon. We didn't want them aboard; we wanted to *own* the bandwagon, and that's what I offered: negotiate an exclusive deal with us, or forget about it. And that's what we got. Our competitors are locked out of this feature, providing us with another sales advantage with prospective customers.

Does this make me an SOB? I doubt it. I suspect every driven businessperson in the same situation would make the same decision; it's easy to be nice when you're successful. But first, you have to be tough.

39

Foster an Epidemic of Enthusiasm

As talented and dedicated as your employees may be, not all of them will be driven to the same degree that you are. Those who share your drive may leave at some point and launch their own business. Your job is to maintain a sufficiently high level of ambition among the balance of your staff. It's a task that driven businesspeople can complete more effectively than traditional managers.

Nothing important in business gets done without a team, and choosing the people to work with me represents one of the biggest challenges of my job. I couldn't expect to find people who thought and acted the way I did. People with those qualifications would be off starting their own businesses. I needed people who both understood my drive and business style, yet brought with them their own unique baskets of skills and knowledge.

Assembling an exceptional team and providing them with the environment to share my goals has been a critical part of both my success and the success of my companies. How did I do it? I wish

I could define the formula I used to guarantee success in selecting and managing employees with the optimum abilities needed for any given job, but I can't. If I could, this would be a very different book directed at a very different audience.

My criteria in choosing employees at key positions have been, for the most part, instinctive. I believe I have the ability, perhaps inherited and sharpened over the years, to recognize hidden talents in people, the ones that rarely appear in resumés and educational records. Much of it is chemistry—can I work alongside this person for eight or ten hours or more a day, day after day? (At least as important is the other side of the question—can they stand working alongside *me* for eight or ten hours a day?) Can I imagine them having fun at this work? Would they remain enthusiastic about their job under pressure? These questions are asked with an open mind, but I must admit that certain qualities influence my judgement somewhat.

I don't need people who believe every business solution resides in a textbook. I need people who accept that life remains unpredictable and challenging and that, when the bullets are flying and the bombs are dropping, the ability to zig and zag is far more valuable than the capacity to figure out the calibre of the bullets and what kinds of planes are flying overhead.

I can almost hear you asking, "If entrepreneurs aren't management types, how do they manage to maximize the contribution of their employees? Doesn't personnel management play a big role in launching and running a company?"

The answer to the second question is clearly yes. The answer to the first question has already been addressed. It's called inspiration.

Woody Allen once said that 80 per cent of success consists of showing up—being there to get the job done, whether it's acting in one of his movies or meeting your sales quota for the month. If you don't show up, you're not even in the game. My philosophy of management is to create a climate so that employees *want* to show up. If you can hardly wait to get to work every morning, almost by definition you'll do a terrific job.

This took a while for me to fully appreciate. In the first several months of running my first company, I was amazed that not everybody shared the same drive as me. My reaction was to apply the Captain Bligh personnel management method—declaring, in effect, "Beatings will continue until morale improves!"

As time passed, I realized this wasn't very effective. Now I try to maintain a different method through various means, and the most important one, as I mentioned earlier, has been not to lead people but to inspire them and generate enthusiasm.

Enthusiasm is contagious. There's nothing like an epidemic of it sweeping through a company to help ensure success in almost any situation. Enthusiasm is also, of course, a common characteristic of entrepreneurs. Anyone who lacks enthusiasm to build something out of nothing but a clear vision and a bucketful of ambition is, by definition, not an entrepreneur. Ensuring that everyone within an organization catches the same enthusiasm for their work eliminates a bunch of personnel management issues on the spot.

The power of enthusiasm cannot be overemphasized. On one episode of *Shark Tank,* enthusiasm alone dispelled my initial scepticism about investing several thousand dollars in a new company.

The company was Grease Monkey Wipes, which I mentioned earlier in this book. Like every other investment opportunity I have encountered on and off the television shows, this one raised a few warning flags for me. Were the young founders really committed to building a successful business over the long term, or were they just dabbling with a dream? Was the product as effective as they claimed? Were they prepared to apply themselves with all the energy the project would require? Would my money be used to build a viable business or to provide perks for the two people pitching for my cash?

Unconvinced, I looked the two young people in the eye and asked a simple and direct question: "Why should I invest in you?"

The young woman who responded to my question did so with so much enthusiasm and passion to succeed that I agreed to the investment. So far, the returns on my money have been spectacular, and I anticipate my investment will continue growing for some time in the future. There really is no substitution for enthusiasm.

You spread enthusiasm in an organization, among other ways, by never asking someone to do something you're not prepared to do yourself. It's all a matter of modelling. If you call a strategy meeting at 6:00 in the morning—yes, I've done that—you must be there at 5:30 and at work when the others arrive. If I told my sales staff that they would each have to sell $100,000 worth of business in the next month, I would make sure that I sold at least $110,000.

I tempered this by keeping a smile on my face at all times, or at least trying to maintain one. I never saw a contradiction between having fun and working hard. I still don't. I'm not sure a smiling boss guarantees enthusiasm, but I'm certain that a constantly scowling boss destroys it.

Another enthusiasm-building technique is to foster an us-against-the-world attitude. I do this by spinning stories of the competition we're operating against, the tricks they may be practising and the unkind things they might be saying about the company.

Everybody wants to belong to something larger than themselves. It's the basis of family loyalty, of cheering for professional sports teams, of political party membership, and of patriotism. It can also represent a motive for everyone going beyond their expectations if the sense of belonging is accompanied by a shared version of changing the world. If you can foster this sense within a positive environment while racking up a series of constant victories, you don't have to be concerned about personnel management issues because, for the most part, there won't be any.

I used to build a sense of teamwork and dedication among my employees with an extension of the "enemy at the gates" concept. Ask employees in other companies who they competed against, and they'll likely stumble through a few names, many of which you may never have heard, with little consistency between them. We always **defined our enemies**. We chose them from the best in the business, and we kept a list of them handy, not as a means of intimidation, but as a source of enthusiasm. Not once did we ever feel that we had no chance of winning against the industry leaders on any given project. We believed that when it came down to performance instead of prominence, we would win every time.

The strategy worked brilliantly in convincing everyone they were part of a first-rate organization that could achieve any goal it set for itself. If you're satisfied with being a second-rate company, you'll choose second-rate competition. We chose the very best, and it made us better.

Don't "Mickey Mouse" Your Customers

Here's what I emphasize to my staff when it comes to dealing with customers at every level in service and sales: Our margin begins the minute you walk through the customer's door.

This is more than the old adage about the need to make a good first impression. Much more. It's about a prevailing positive attitude maintained by everyone in your company. The attitude is communicated by the way our company representatives dress, talk, listen and respond to a customer's concerns. Overriding all of these is the sense of pride and ownership that employees have about their company, because these qualities influence how well they conduct themselves in the customers' eyes and how successful the company will be in its operations.

This last point was delivered with great impact by Michael Eisner at a business seminar I attended a few years ago. Eisner was CEO of the Walt Disney Company at the time, and he identified pride of ownership as one of the keys to the company's success.

"We have about 120,000 employees at Disney, including our parks," Eisner told us. Then he asked: "Of that number, how many do you think are responsible for maintenance, including picking up garbage and noting where something needs cleaning or painting?"

Eisner went around the room asking for estimates. Somebody guessed eight hundred, somebody else suggested ten thousand, and others tossed out similar numbers.

Finally, Eisner gave the correct answer: "It's 120,000. Every Disney employee in every division at every level is expected to act on anything they encounter that fails to match our standards of perfection."

Every customer encounter with Disney, Eisner explained, was called an M.O.M.—a Moment of Magic. Whether it was shaking hands with Mickey Mouse, boarding a ride at a theme park or purchasing a souvenir, the M.O.M. would not occur if it were spoiled by a piece of garbage on the ground or an attraction that needed a coat of paint. Disney employees know this and are encouraged to take action themselves. Thus Eisner's claim of having 120,000 maintenance workers on staff.

This was a classic "aha!" moment for me, and since then I've attempted to create a similar environment in any company I managed.

It's all about creating a sense of pride in your organization and an environment in which everyone will do whatever is required—not because you are forcing them, but because they are proud of the place where they work. In my company, we don't print anyone's job title on their business cards, and we never have. Every now and then, a new employee, or someone working for a company we buy, will ask about that. We explain that we do this because it is anyone's job to do whatever it takes. That's not a corny, pat statement of belief—it's an essential part of our culture.

40

If They Can't Catch You, They Can't Squash You

No company is too large to fail. General Motors proved this rule, if proof were needed. GM's problems didn't begin with the recession of 2008. The roots of its troubles can be traced back to the 1970s and 1980s, when the company ignored challenges from upstarts like Honda and Toyota. By moving faster than the North American automakers in technological and styling advances, the Japanese companies first caught, then passed and almost squashed, GM, Ford and Chrysler.

The auto companies represent an extreme example, but the lesson applies to companies of every size in every field: if you are not prepared to run hard, be prepared either to drop out of the race or be flattened.

Remember my advice about training for a marathon but being prepared for a sprint? If you've come this far in the book, you know that the race is always a sprint. This is especially true of small companies competing in markets driven by fast-changing technology and dominated by giants. Or, to bring back another earlier analogy, the little guys are mice and the giants are elephants. The mice are relatively safe as long as they keep moving. In that situation, a slow mouse is soon a squashed mouse.

You've heard this before, but that doesn't make it any less true: in business, you either keep growing, or you die. When you cease to grow, your company will either slowly starve to death because other mice have gobbled all the food, or will move slowly enough to be flattened under an elephant's foot.

If you have the drive and vision to battle the odds and start a new company based on your vision and ambition, don't let up. Keep moving and growing, and someday perhaps you'll join the elephants in size and power. Then you can enjoy squishing the slow-moving mice.

Make the Telephone Ring

The more specialized your potential market is, the more focused your activity must be on making the telephone ring. By "activity" I mean more than advertising and promotion; I mean making cold telephone calls, using well-written e-mails, creating an effective website and so on. Activity generates activity. It spreads, it breeds, it inspires and, if you have the right combination of price, product and performance, it sells.

I know of no secrets to prospecting for business except that, whatever technique is selected, it must be framed by the nature of your industry and the market you serve. As a supplier of Internet security services, my company has limited potential from traditional trade advertising. Our expansion is based on

constantly expanding and replenishing our customer base, supported, for the most part, by old-fashioned cold calls and effective networking.

Driving these activities are two factors: the acceptance that it is
our responsibility to track and successfully promote our services
to potential customers; and a proactive attitude that recognizes
our own responsibility to build our business.

That's how you make the telephone ring. Not by assuming customers will perform the work of pursuing you for your business,
but by assuming the responsibility yourself. If the sweetest sound
in business is hearing a cash register ring (figuratively speaking),
the second-sweetest is hearing the telephone ring in response to
your efforts to build business volume.

41

Never Accept the First Offer

I have often heard entrepreneurs or business owners refer to their companies as "my baby." I understand that it's meant to describe the fondness or the proprietary aspect of an organization they have created and nurtured, but the term makes me uncomfortable. I believe it also colours the decision-making process if the owner is approached by a potential buyer.

Your children are your babies. Your business is your business. A distinct line exists between them. Every business has a price. Your family hasn't.

As someone who values the well-being of his family above all else, I know who "my babies" are, and even when the term is loosely used in conjunction with a corporation, the reference makes me uneasy. True, corporations are often likened to living, breathing organisms in many ways, an analogy that is useful in managing and diagnosing growth and challenges, but in my case I do not consider my company to be an extension of my life, or even my legacy. My legacy will be my children, and what they achieve and represent in their own lives.

On a more practical note, the same kind of attitude that inspires someone to refer to a corporation as "my baby" may blind them to the economic wisdom of selling their firm for a profit if and when the opportunity arises.

There are risks to that decision, of course, but risks are hardly new to entrepreneurs and most independent businesspeople. The major risk involves a driven entrepreneur facing an empty calendar the day after he or she sells the company they have built over many years. What do they do now? Most, armed with a treasure trove of cash, look for other worlds to conquer, other corporations to launch.

The sale of a company, if the payment qualifies as a capital gain in Canada, generates an enormous tax advantage to the seller. Half of every capital gain earned in Canada is free of income tax. Sell your company for $10 million more than your original investment and, if the tax gods continue to smile upon you, $5 million will be free of income tax.

The impact of an eight-figure profit on your family, assuming you are relatively free of personal debts at the time, can be life-changing. Whether the change is for better or worse is determined by other factors, especially the values you have inculcated to your children. These are facts to be pondered by every entrepreneur whose corporate creation finds itself the object of a buyout. Do you lose your "baby," or do you decide to sell and make a positive (you hope) impact on your children and grandchildren? I sold my company for the latter reason, and I have absolutely no regrets.

A Personal Case Study of Successful Selling

People employed in the mergers and acquisitions (M&A) departments of giant corporations fascinate me. They're all very bright and highly educated, socially secure and well dressed, can mix a great martini, all of that. But I have yet to meet one who has ever started, managed or sold a business. These people can read every semicolon in an annual report and every legal clause in a contract, but how good are they at reading the inner feelings of the person who launched the company they set out to acquire?

M&A people are essential to billion-dollar corporations because the companies frequently are unable to launch new divisions on their own, even when the new division's function is directly related to their core service. The people who run these large, well-established companies have little in common with entrepreneurs. Most sparks of innovation that shone within the company when it was small and hungry faded long ago. When it comes to truly new ideas, these large firms have to buy the fire somewhere else.

I didn't launch my company to participate directly in the Internet connectivity business. Other companies provided that service and had been operating merrily and profitably for some time. It was after launching my firm that I saw a need for security from an angle that the companies supplying the connections couldn't perceive. That's when we focused our activity on providing Internet security services for customers.

When the full impact of the Internet was finally assessed and people began to recognize that the game had changed entirely, security providers like us became hot. At firms all across North

America executives looked around, said, "We need to protect our Internet customers with an effective security system," and dispatched M&A people to find a company that was doing the job well. Many of them found us.

I began receiving tentative invitations to dance with suitors who had deep pockets, but I didn't take the offers seriously until the telephone companies came calling. Their pockets were far deeper and their desperation to deal with security concerns more evident than the others. Providing security to their customers was like installing indoor plumbing in a new house; they wanted it done correctly and quickly, with little regard for the cost.

Most of the enquiries I received were easy to shrug off because the valuations were too low and the prospects for my staff were not promising. If I were to sell my company, it had to be for an exceptional amount of money to a company that would provide job security and a good working environment for my employees.

When an offer arrived from AT&T Canada, a wholly owned subsidiary of its U.S. parent, I treated it seriously. My interest grew stronger after meeting several of AT&T's key people. I liked the CEO, and his M&A team were friendly and persuasive. Much of their pitch to me dealt with rolling my company into AT&T as an entire division, assuring me that my employees would still have jobs after the deal was completed. Beyond that, it came down to the question of price. At a basic level, it was almost like selling a new car to a wealthy buyer. I had a vehicle they wanted, they had money to pay for it, and we both had to agree on the amount of money to be exchanged.

The Only Person Who Can Truly Estimate the Value of a Company Is the One Buying It

I had built my company in a conservative fashion, taking an immigrant's approach to financing. I was always concerned about protecting my personal investment, following an old-fashioned philosophy of never creating more debt than you can justify and easily service. I'm not sure of the origins of this policy—perhaps Europe's generations of upheaval made immigrants from there more sensitive to risk than North Americans—but the result was a healthy company that would pass any standard accountancy test for value as a going concern.

On that basis, I expected AT&T's M&A people to work out the usual cluster of ratios and assessments, perhaps questioning me on income estimates, depreciation and other items that accountants toss around. Eventually, I assumed, someone would apply a mathematical formula to find my company's market value and make me a carefully calculated offer.

But they didn't. The price that AT&T Canada would be offering, I was informed, would be based not on its book value but on its sales revenue. "We'll be calculating our offer as a multiple of your annual gross income," one of the M&A team members told me.

I wasn't sure I had heard him correctly. How can you make an offer based on a company's revenue alone, ignoring all the other aspects of operating a business? I heard no reference to our operating expenses or that favourite bean-counter's metric, EBITDA (earnings before interest, taxes, depreciation and amortization). Without assessing expenses, how would you know if—let alone when—you could expect to get your money back?

It took me a while to realize the answer. The value of my company as a going concern was irrelevant to them. AT&T's primary concern centred on the scope of our business and the degree of customer satisfaction we were producing, which they could pass along to their customers immediately by purchasing my firm. The move would vault them into a dominant market position where security was concerned, and that was their primary objective. In that light, the time it took to get their money back was not a factor. At least, that's how it seemed to me, but I had to make certain, so I called the M&A group leader.

"Just to make this clear," I said to him, "you will be basing your offer on a multiple of my annual revenue, is that correct?"

He replied with one word: "Yes."

When I called my wife, Diane, to tell her I was selling the business, she almost didn't believe me. "How can you know it after one meeting?" she asked. "You haven't heard the details."

I didn't care about the details. They were paying me a multiple of our revenue. It didn't matter what that multiple was; any offer based entirely on revenue would be acceptable to me.

The entire AT&T team attended the negotiation meetings, including the M&A specialists, lawyers, accountants and other people whose roles I never fully understood. I counted about twenty people at their end of the boardroom table. I sat facing them, alone, at the other end. I didn't need a team of specialists, all of whom would have shared the same MBA-style thinking as the people on the other side. Not at the outset, anyway.

None of the M&A people had ever launched a company on their credit card, slept on the office floor overnight, mortgaged everything they owned to keep the firm afloat for a week, or powered themselves through difficult times solely on their dreams and ambition. None of them ever would, and they knew it. They were, to some degree, in awe of me for doing all of that and more. I was an unusual species to them, somebody whose life was so removed from their own that they couldn't imagine living it.

They would perform due diligence before things were finalized, I knew, and I was happy with that. Some of my own staff boasted MBAs, and the AT&T people could associate with them when they went looking under the covers of the company for problems.

That would come later. For now, they remained a little intrigued with me, which gave me a negotiating advantage and balanced the twenty-to-one odds somewhat.

Prepare to Bargain Hard

After a short exchange of pleasantries, the team from AT&T Canada submitted their offer. The price was good. In fact, it was *very* good, and I would have been thrilled to accept it. It was more money than I had ever imagined earning in my entire life.

I turned it down.

I feared that if I accepted their first offer, they might grow suspicious. I had nothing to hide, but neither did I want AT&T to believe I was anxious for them to take the company off my hands. Besides, I don't believe in ever accepting the first offer in a negotiation, because rejecting it strengthens your bargaining position. They would raise their offer, I expected, and they did. First, they asked for a counter-offer from me, and I quoted a figure twice the size of theirs.

I neither hoped nor expected that AT&T would pay that amount, but I believed they would return with a price somewhere in between. They did, and their new offer was comfortably higher than their original one. After some feigned consideration, I agreed to accept the new price, which was substantially more than their first offer.

The amount of money represented not just a measure of all I had achieved in building my company to its leadership position, it represented a generational change, money that would affect the lives of Diane and me as well as the lives of our children and their children. You can spend your entire life working for a seven-figure salary and, if you are talented, hard-working and lucky, you might accumulate a few million dollars in total income. But this wasn't income; this was a massive amount of capital falling directly into my lap.

AT&T's due diligence went without a hitch as expected, the contracts were signed, and in time the cheque was issued. Was I pleased? Of course I was, in one sense. Yet as much as I acknowledged the impact the deal would have on my family and the personal pride I took in generating a substantial personal net worth, one thought kept running through my mind as I added my signature to the deal: *I wish I had enough money of my own to turn this offer down . . .*

A Guide to Selling Your Company

- **It's flattering, but . . .** Be cautious about selling your current company if you expect to start a new one to replace it. First, you will almost certainly be restricted from competing with your old firm. Second, success with one company does not ensure success with another. In effect, you are expecting lightning to strike twice in the same place. Accept that the odds are against you.

- **Ideally, sell only if the earnings will change your life and your family's life.** Again, you may be expecting too much to assume that you can move from your current business to an entirely new one with equal success. Whatever profit you can take from this business should be so impressive that you don't need the new business, if any, to succeed. Of course, you may be so driven that you couldn't imagine not succeeding at a new venture. In which case . . .

- **Maximize your company's value.** Some people believe in buying other companies during economic difficulties when values are at their lowest. I disagree. I would prefer to purchase a firm when it is doing well and use that momentum to construct even greater financial success. Otherwise, you're buying a problem. From a seller's point of view, it makes sense to market your company when you have taken it as far as you can go, subject to the two earlier points.

- **I also believe it is better to pay well for a good company than to get a bad company at a discount.** Once a boulder starts rolling down the hill it is very difficult to stop—not impossible, true, but difficult. I would rather get involved with a boulder that is on flat ground or a slight uphill grade, because with my effort and knowledge I can get it over the hump and start accelerating and gaining momentum.

- **We all have different skills, and different degrees of those skills.** Some of us can take a company to extremely high values in terms of sales and assets. Others become mired in management difficulties at a much lower valuation. When you become mired, consider selling your business.
- **One more time: never accept the first offer.** You may have one opportunity in life to be awarded a lump sum of cash as a return on all your hard work as a business owner and manager. Try to capitalize on any opportunity to put a few more dollars in your pocket.

42

Listen to Your Heroes

After my experience in Silicon Valley, I returned home to spend three years as a stay-at-home father, delighting in the company of my children. This was remarkable for a guy as driven as me. I value the role of a parent as much as anything we can do with our lives, but it did not, after all, involve the skills I had used to create a company from nothing more than a concept and build it into a financial success.

When all my children were in full-time attendance at school I decided it was time to become an entrepreneur again, launching a new company serving the Internet-based computer industry.

I could have begun as basically a one-man show, opening an office somewhere and dividing my time between seeking clients and recruiting key personnel. Talented people are not uncommon in the computer technology industry, but talented people who shared my vision and boasted a proven record of achievement were rare.

I had a team, a vision, a management philosophy and a solid source of investment capital—my own.

The Herjavec Group officially opened its doors in 2002 as a three-person firm combining what we believed to be the best blend of technology, products and service in the computer services field. Following a difficult first year, we gained traction and began to thrive to the point where various business magazines and organizations recognized us as one of the fastest-growing companies in the IT field.

That measure of success was reached by way of a much different approach than the one I had used with my earlier companies. I launched The Herjavec Group with the same determination, but shaped it in a different manner. Some might claim I have mellowed. I prefer to call it a change in emphasis.

The Herjavec Group was launched not out of a need to earn a living but from a challenge I set for myself and, in a fashion, for everyone within the firm. The challenge was to create a company that set standards not exclusively for financial performance, although that's as vital as any other measure. I wanted to set an exceptional standard of excellence within my industry, a level of quality in service and performance that no one else could equal.

This sounds like corporate boasting, the kind of language you encounter in a promotional brochure. I had a model in mind, however, an example of what can be achieved by setting standards above everyone else in your field and meeting them.

My model was Issy Sharp's vision for the Four Seasons hotel chain, which he started from a small motel on Toronto's Jarvis Street. Sharp's goal was not to build the biggest hotel chain in the world or even the most profitable or fastest growing. His goal was to build the *greatest* hotel chain in the world. I loved that concept, and

I decided to apply it to The Herjavec Group. Unlike Four Seasons, you won't find our offices in exotic locations around the world, of course, and it's impossible to compare the qualities that make Four Seasons such an acknowledged leader in the hotel field with the ones we're using to build our company. But they both operate with the same manner of thinking. We want to be the best in our field, without question. And we both accept the fact that achieving excellence in customer service is not a destination, it is a journey.

Accumulating wealth is only one measure of being driven. A similar energy drives people who earn my admiration for their success in fields far removed from business—people such as Dr. Amit Oza.

Dr. Oza's professional background is impressive. It includes a medical degree from the University of London in the U.K. and fellowships at St. Bartholomew's Hospital in London and the Netherlands Cancer Institute in Amsterdam. He is currently a senior staff physician and professor of medicine at Princess Margaret Hospital, which is affiliated with the University of Toronto. His clinical research work on cancer, especially gynecological cancer and advanced colorectal malignancies, resulted in some of the most advanced and effective treatments to be developed.

I met Dr. Oza when he was treating my mother for the cancer that eventually took her life. I recognized a similar drive in Dr. Oza, a purity of purpose I have seen in successful businesspeople. It's a mindset, an attitude that drives everything they do, and their achievements inspire countless people of their own and future generations to emulate their success.

Without their drive, the world would be a lesser place in so many ways, and Dr. Oza has become one of my heroes, someone whose skill, dedication and drive represent a model for me and perhaps for others.

Here are just some of my business heroes (in no particular order):

Rebecca MacDonald

I could be accused of favouritism here because, like me, Rebecca emigrated from Yugoslavia to Canada without understanding more than a few words of English. She married Pearson MacDonald, who emphasized the importance of sales in every business venture. This led first to a career with Avon, selling cosmetics door to door, and later to selling and promoting natural gas through her company, Energy Marketing Inc. After the sudden death of her husband in 1992, she continued building her business, which she sold in 1995 before starting Energy Savings L.P. By 2010, doing business throughout Canada and the United States, that company had annual sales of $1.7 billion.

My favourite quote from Rebecca: "The only way you can be successful is by constantly raising the bar. We didn't start this company thinking we would have sales of over $1.5 billion. We started one customer at a time. So, you get a hundred and say, 'Why can't I get a thousand, or ten thousand or a hundred thousand?' We all start small but you can't think small over a long period of time."

Ron Joyce

He abandoned a career as a police officer to lease an abandoned gas station in a rough neighbourhood of Hamilton, Ontario, which he converted into a coffee and donut shop named for his partner and source of venture capital: Tim Horton. Like Issy Sharp, Ron is both a visionary and a builder, a man who could have stopped at one donut shop, or a dozen or a hundred, but was driven to build the company into an economic powerhouse and a cultural phenomenon.

My favourite quote from Ron Joyce: "When you find the niche you love, that becomes your passion. For me, it was Tim Hortons. It was my world."

Michael Dell

Here is the classic example of a successful, driven entrepreneur who never wanted to build a better mousetrap. He had little to do with the launch and development of the personal computer, yet influenced the industry in more ways than almost anyone else and, almost incidentally, built a personal fortune of more than $12 billion through Dell Inc., the first computer company to build and ship products on demand. He launched and ran the firm from his university dorm and managed to have his company listed on the Nasdaq stock exchange when he was just twenty-three years old.

My favourite quote from Michael Dell: "There's a whole lot of winning left to happen. You can find markets where we're number one, but I like the markets where we're not number one, and I can name lots of them."

Larry Ellison

Like Dell, Ellison did not graduate from university, leaving after his second year. In the mid-1970s, while working on a database project for the CIA with Ampex Corporation, Ellison recognized the need for computer programs that could store and access enormous amounts of information quickly and accurately. The project was code-named Oracle, and with $1,400 of his own money he launched the company now know as Oracle Corporation as a software supporter of IBM systems. When IBM refused to cooperate, Ellison developed his own programs, which proved a brilliant move. Over the years, Ellison built Oracle into a global powerhouse (and his personal wealth to $22 billion) despite serious economic, legal and competitive challenges.

My favourite quote from Larry Ellison: "All you can do every day is try to solve a problem and make your company better. You can't worry about it, you can't panic when you look at the stock market's decline, or you get frozen like a deer in the headlights. All you can do is all you can do."

43

Why You Shouldn't Pay Yourself the Most

Beyond the pride of creating a profitable entity out of little more than a vision, how should the founder of a company be compensated for the hard work behind his or her creation?

If you reply, "With the biggest salary in the company," you're wrong. For a number of reasons, the entrepreneur's tangible reward should be in the equity created within the operation, not the annual salary paid. Owners who build and hang onto as much equity as possible rather than maximizing their salaries ultimately earn bigger rewards and tend to have better functioning companies.

Whenever I investigate purchasing a private company, I ask the owner to name the highest-paid person in the firm. Typically, the owner replies, "I am." If I hear this, my opinion of the venture drops dramatically. But if the owner says the highest-paid employee is a salesperson who brings in the largest volume of business, or a programming engineer who writes the complex codes behind the company's success, I realize I'm talking to someone who understands that the true value of ownership is equity, not salary, and almost certainly is a more effective executive.

As for employee compensation in general, my approach is to keep it simple and follow the rule that average employees are paid at average income levels and exceptional people earn exceptional salaries.

This confuses prospective new employees at The Herjavec Group. Hearing our salary offer, they may comment, "You know, I could make more money achieving my target productivity at another company." My response is to show them our bonus program and ask, "And if you achieve your target plus x, as shown here, could you make this amount of money anywhere else?" The answer is inevitably no.

The company's compensation structure is skewed towards incentives. Make 125 per cent of your quota at The Herjavec Group and you'll make twice as much as someone at 123 per cent of quota. The intent is to push people to a place where they may not otherwise feel comfortable going.

Does this put pressure on the employees? Definitely, but it's positive pressure. Imagine the pressure on someone who has achieved 123 per cent of quota, and who knows that just another two percentage points' worth of successful effort will double their income.

People are rarely fired in our company. Employees quickly figure out whether or not they can handle the atmosphere. If they are unable to deal with it, they choose to leave on their own. Those who can handle the pressure not only thrive individually but feed off each other. When five out of twenty people succeed in doubling their income as a result of exceeding their quota by 25 per cent, the remaining employees begin asking themselves, why can't it be me?

How to Find Out whether a Company Is Dynamic

Here's my guide for an ambitious person seeking employment with a dynamic company. Before your interview, check out the cars in the company parking lot. Look for brands like Mercedes-Benz, Lexus, Porsche, BMWs and so on. How many do you see? Toyotas and Hondas are fine cars, but if almost everyone in the company drives one (assuming, of course, that the company isn't Toyota or Honda), what does that tell you about the income level? Note the most expensive car you see. Perhaps it's a Ferrari. Then, during the job interview, ask who owns it. If the only luxury vehicle belongs to the owner, think twice about working for that firm.

You might also pay attention to the company's facilities, although these may reflect the nature of the firm's business as much as the owner/CEO's value system. If the company, for example, is engaged in servicing heavy industry, its location may coincide with that of at least some of its primary customers. As much as the location, consider the facilities' size and decor. Everyone enjoys working in an atmosphere of luxury and comfort, but money spent on frills and bragging rights is money not available to employees and shareholders. One of the first clues that Enron, the U.S. energy conglomerate that collapsed in 2001, was being mismanaged was the creation of its enormous and luxurious Houston headquarters. In Canada, the downfall of insurance giant Confederation Life was in part precipitated, according to many observers, by the construction of its over-the-top headquarters.

I take the view that employees represent a special breed of customers to the firms that employ them. In that respect, they deserve a pleasant, comfortable working environment. The problems arise when the owners and CEOs of successful companies begin viewing the firm's facilities not as a workplace but as a monument to their success and to themselves.

After inspecting the cars in the parking lot, stop and think about the money invested in the workplace. Who is the investment really serving—you, the company's clients or the egos of the top brass? And if it's the latter, what does this tell you about them?

Businesses often fail when the owner insists on having both the biggest salary and maximum equity, sometimes augmented by excessive spending on extravagant goodies. You can't do it all effectively, and the most successful private businesses I've encountered recognize this fact. Owners should invest in facilities that emphasize comfort and efficiency over indulgence and ego stroking, pay the largest salaries to the people most responsible for the firm's success, and convert that success into equity, holding on to as much of it as possible for as long as possible.

44

Fly Your Hopes, but Walk Your Expectations

One of the biggest errors made by pitchers on *Dragons' Den* is their conviction that they will build their idea into an immense success within a tiny amount of time. When I or one of the other panel members question their estimate of the net worth of their company, these pitchers often reply that they expect to quickly expand by a factor of two or ten. "In a few years, this will be gigantic!" they promise, if not in so many words.

I dislike raining on anyone's parade, but where my money is concerned, I insist on realism. The suggestion that your business idea, worth little more today than whatever amount of cash is in your pocket, will be valued in the millions within a couple of years is as foolish as believing you'll win next week's lottery because your neighbour won this week. Yes, it's possible; but stop every now and then to give yourself a cold shower of reality.

Let's consider $50 million in annual revenue as an acceptable measure of gigantic success for your new venture. That's a lot of money, although we're talking revenue, not profit. For a company operating as a national entity, or hoping to become one, it shouldn't be an impossible target.

How long did it take some of the most successful companies in our time to reach that level? Here are a notable few.

- **Microsoft.** The world's largest, wealthiest and in many ways most powerful corporation rang up almost $61 billion in sales in 2008. Founded in 1975, Microsoft took a full eight years before it reached a comparatively paltry $50 million in annual revenue in 2009 dollars.
- **Oracle.** Two years after Microsoft's launch, Oracle came along, and in 2008 it scored $22.4 billion in sales. That's a hefty figure, but the rise was slow. It took a full ten years for Oracle's annual revenue to reach the $50 million mark.
- **Roots.** It's a Canadian clothing icon now, but the manufacturer and retailer with almost two hundred stores around the world took an estimated ten years to reach $50 million in sales (Roots is a private company and sales figures are estimated from industry sources).

In the same year that each of these companies saw the first light of day, untold thousands of other outfits—many launched by people whose intelligence and drive were comparable to those of Bill Gates, Larry Ellison, Michael Budman and Don Green—also were founded and have long since vanished.

Should this dissuade you from launching your own start-up company? That's not my intention. I do hope, however, to influence you to be reasonable in your expectations of success and the degree of rewards it may bring. Fly your enthusiasm in the clouds, but walk your probabilities on the ground. Things are more solid there.

You shouldn't focus on the odds that are stacked up against you, I'll admit. If everyone believed they were likely to fail, no one would take the first step towards success. Just don't divorce yourself from reality by believing your business will burst into an enormous money machine overnight.

Believing in yourself and your idea is fine, but it would be helpful to have a guiding principle to alert you to common dangers. Here's one I suggest: **you will always overestimate what you can achieve in one year and underestimate what you will achieve in ten years.**

As critical as enthusiasm may be, it can lead to excessive expectations in your first year of operations. The first few orders you receive may trigger visions of yachts and Caribbean getaways. Dream if you must, but these things will almost certainly remain fantasies based on a single year in business. So much must be achieved in a company's first few years that, even if you become as successful as you hope, you'll be too busy establishing your firm as a long-term entity to put your feet up and relax for several weeks at a time. Or, at least, you should be. That same kind of work ethic, however, creates long-term success.

Watch for Speed Bumps on the Road to Your Goal

Sometimes the most enlightening wisdom we receive in life is also the most basic. Like, "People who enjoy their work always do a better job." You can see this among entrepreneurs who are driven to succeed, not to become wealthy—not immediately, anyway—but because they enjoy it. They enjoy the challenge, the chaos, the creativity of it all. This may explain why many people who launch businesses fail. If your solitary goal is to become wealthy, you're doing it out of greed, not out of love. If you do not honestly love what you do, maybe you should be doing something else. But if your career represents a major source of joy in each day of your life, you're a lap or two ahead of other people on the same track.

I try to make the people in my company as enthusiastic about showing up every morning as I am. That's impossible, but we still try to have fun—there's that word again.

I don't want anyone on my payroll grumbling about the company. People who take the company's name in vain forget that it feeds them and their families. Yes, they may disagree with me from time to time, and in fact they do. But disagreeing with the top guy shouldn't translate into dissatisfaction with the entire organization.

Managing, as I noted earlier, is almost never one of the prime talents of entrepreneurs. To truly succeed in launching and maintaining your own business, you need two kinds of vision. One is for long distances, helping you keep your eye on the goal you have set, the one that's somewhere at the end of the road you're travelling on. The other type of vision helps you recognize the speed bumps ten feet in front of you—the ones that will throw you into the ditch if you overlook them.

I doubt that knowing that most start-up companies do not survive beyond their fifth year of operation will dissuade truly driven businesspeople. Far higher odds against success do not prevent millions of Canadians from buying lottery tickets every week.

Of course, business is not a lottery. Many—perhaps most—people launching a start-up company are investing, not just a few loonies each week in the hope of becoming wealthy, but much of their entire net worth into a venture they believe in.

A study issued in 2009 by New York University[2] plotted the survival rate of several thousand businesses founded in 1998 over the next seven years, according to the nature of the business each was serving. In all the categories covered, ranging from natural resources and construction through financial services and leisure activities, barely 38 per cent were still in operation five years later. I find it interesting that the highest survival rate—just over half of the companies surveyed—was recorded by companies in the health services field, and the lowest rate was scored by information and data-based firms, which is my field. Five years after they were launched, only three out of ten new companies providing information services were still around; after seven years this had declined to one in four.

The survey, limited to U.S. companies, did not identify the primary reason for failure in each category, but I suspect the two factors behind the high failure rate for I.T./data firms were intense competition and inexperience. Over the past decade, no business sector in North America has grown as quickly and drawn as many

2 Aswath Damodaran, "Valuing Young, Start-up and Growth Companies: Estimation Issues and Valuation Challenges," Stern School of Business, New York University, 2009.

eager entrepreneurs as information services. The entry of more players into the game raises the odds against winning.

In addition, the fast-paced technological side of the business attracted a higher proportion of younger players determined to become the next Bill Gates, Michael Dell or Larry Ellison based almost exclusively on their technical expertise and enthusiasm. Enthusiasm is valuable in launching a business. Enthusiasm plus wisdom and experience is priceless.

Top Ten Reasons Why New Companies Fail Within Five Years

One of the most valuable assets any entrepreneur can have is a positive outlook. It enables them to focus on why their new company will grow into one of the great success stories in business history rather than falling into the lengthy list of failures.

There are various reasons why some companies survive and others cost their owners immense loss and heartbreak. After reviewing a host of studies on the subject, I have narrowed these down to the ten most common. Some companies fail as a result of just one of these errors or weaknesses; for others, multiple causes came into play. I suspect that the companies that made it past the five-year mark managed to avoid all or most of the pitfalls on the list.

1. **Lack of management skills.** This appears to be the number one reason for failure—no expertise in finance, sales, production and employee management. If you lack these abilities, either hire someone capable of providing them or acquire them yourself before launching your venture.

2. **Started for the wrong reasons.** Launching your own business as a means of making a lot of money in a short time, or hoping you'll have more time to spend with your family, invites failure. If you don't have the passion, you won't have the motivation to succeed. It's as simple as that.

3. **Neglect by the founder/top executive.** As far as I know, no business functions on autopilot. To thrive, grow and even survive requires constant attention from the individual guiding the enterprise.

4. **Ineffective leadership.** This involves effective hiring and personnel management, an emphasis on training and motivation, forward vision and strategic thinking, and the ability to inspire everyone around you. Companies lacking these elements are merely coasting—and coasting, as you know, is only achieved by going downhill.

5. **Insufficient capital.** Many entrepreneurs underestimate the amount of money a business requires during its first year of operation while overestimating the sales and profit it will record. Take a cold, hard look at the expenses involved in starting a company and maintaining it over the first year or two.

6. **Poor location.** This usually affects retail operations, which need proximity to their customers as well as ease of accessibility and parking. But location can also hamper service and technological firms related to the Internet that are intent on attracting skilled employees. Assuming you can handle the overhead costs, you won't have trouble attracting top computer-based professionals if you're based in California's Silicon Valley or in Waterloo, Ontario. You will have a much

more difficult time attracting them if, for example, you're based in Moosomin, Saskatchewan.

7. **Poor planning.** Dreams are wonderful assets for those launching start-up businesses, but they are totally impractical when plotting day-to-day, month-to-month and year-to-year decisions. Preparing a business plan forces you to articulate and focus on the steps needed to realize a dream, as well as providing a means for you to reassess and revise your thinking as time passes.

8. **Expanding too far and too soon.** Growth is essential to every business, but unplanned and unwarranted growth can be fatal. Ensure that productivity and financial resources, among other items, are in place before embarking on an expansion program.

9. **Lack of energy and motivation.** This one is frequently overlooked and usually unacknowledged. Running your own business does not provide instant entry into a life of leisure— quite the opposite, in fact. Long working hours, stress and poor diet can challenge anyone whose physical and mental conditions are less than first-rate. This is one reason most business owners and top executives devote a portion of their time to improving and maintaining their physical condition. Facing a series of ten-, twelve- or fourteen-hour days is challenging even when you love what you do. It's far easier if you maintain both your physical and mental energy, enabling you to make faster and better decisions.

10. **Lack of honesty and integrity.** It all comes down to trust— trust that you can succeed by being fair and honest in all your

business transactions, and trust that, with reasonable care on your part, others will treat you will equal fairness. True, disappointments and losses may occur. But most companies that cannot maintain expected levels of integrity stand to lose their reputations and their customers.

45

Keep Your Eyes Fixed on the Road Ahead

Lessons in life and business can be acquired anywhere. Many of the things that shaped me as a person and as a businessman I can trace back to my childhood in Croatia, waiting tables in Yorkville and working at a collection agency. Sometimes the lessons were clear and specific; other times they were more subtle and wide-ranging but valuable nevertheless. Like the lesson I learned from auto racing.

I have a passion for fast cars. There's no logic to wanting a vehicle that can travel three times as fast as the maximum legal speed limit or that costs as much as the average suburban house. You either get it or you don't, and when it comes to powerful sports cars, I get it in a big way.

When my income could justify the expense, I gave into my craving to own a fast car, something smoother and more sophisticated than my Corvette. Naturally, it was a Ferrari—a red 1986 Testarossa, one of the sexiest cars ever made. With its twelve-cylinder high-performance engine rumbling like an angry bear, the car never failed to attract attention.

Ferraris, of course, are not designed to cruise city streets. They're made to carve corners on racetracks at speeds in excess of 160 kilometres an hour. One day, I took the Testarossa to a track where I thought I might test its performance and my driving skill. It happened that a professional race driver had brought his own Ferrari to the track to put through its paces, and I watched him tear around the track at top speed until, on one of the curves, he lost control and totalled his car against a wall.

He hadn't been in an actual race, just curious to see what he and his car could do when not restricted by highway laws. Nevertheless, the incident happened on a racetrack, not a public highway, and auto insurance companies take a dim view of their policyholders driving expensive machines anywhere except on a public road. As a result, the unfortunate driver whose million-dollar Ferrari became an instant write-off would have a difficult time persuading his insurance company to cover any of the car's value.

"Never race anything you can't afford to walk away from," a friend commented after the crash. He wasn't referring to the financial impact of a crash. He meant the near-impossibility of winning a race with that attitude. If your major concern is preserving the value of the car you're driving, you will never race to the limit of your ability—you will race to the limit of your pocketbook.

It was a dramatic lesson, but it failed to discourage me from investing in my own race car and testing my own driving skills. As it turned out, the decision tested my survival skills and sharpened my business instincts.

The Complex Power of the Mind

I began looking around for an opportunity to test whether my passion for driving at speeds close to two hundred kilometres per hour was as powerful as my passion for business. I chose Formula Vee, a class of racing in high-powered, open-wheeled cars that resemble Formula One and Indy cars in appearance and handling, but are comparably inexpensive—a word that rarely appears in the same sentence with automobile racing.

Formula Vee attracts two kinds of drivers: young people, some still in their teens, who have enough skill to earn sponsorship, perhaps on their way to Indy circuits, and older folk like me, usually men in their forties who can afford the investment and who believe that, had they been given the chance twenty years earlier, they just might have become a competitive race driver on the fastest tracks in the world. For this group, the category might have been labelled "Second Chance" racing.

Despite the age range, Formula Vee is serious racing. I worked hard to win my racing licence, and during my first year I actually competed against Jacques Villeneuve, whose father, Gilles, had been a top Formula One driver and who demonstrated similar driving skills and competitive spirit. (Jacques went on to win the 1995 IndyCar championship, and became the Formula One world champion in 1997.)

Competitive racing teaches you one thing above all, and that's the complex power of your mind. When it comes to survival instincts, the mind proves more powerful than the body. Here's an example: you enter a corner at two hundred kilometres an hour and the car begins to spin. Ahead of you, as the car slides along the track, is a wall. You don't want to hit the wall for a dozen different reasons, ranging from losing the race to potentially losing your life. The normal human reaction is to look at the wall; the wall is a threat to be avoided at all costs. In racing, you are taught never to look at the wall, because if you do you will surely hit it, no matter how hard you try to avoid it. That's because during the few milliseconds it takes to absorb the message—*Omigod, I'm going to hit the wall!*—your hands will freeze on the steering wheel.

Experienced drivers learn to avoid looking at the wall and fix their eyes instead on where they want to go, which is down the track ahead of them. In other words, you train your mind to remain focused on where you want to go and not where you actually appear to be going. This sounds to me like a pretty good analogy for doing business in a competitive climate—look away from the danger and towards the opportunity. Or, if you prefer, keep your eye on your objective and avoid staring at the wall.

Other racing lessons don't adapt themselves to business quite so easily, although they do illustrate the risks of some instinctive actions. When an open-wheeled, open-cockpit car flips, for example, the driver's head and body are generally protected by seat belts and roll bars. The biggest risk of injury concerns the driver's arms, since the driver's instinct is to throw his or her arms out to protect themselves. Do this in a race car about to flip onto its back and both of your arms will be crushed. To avoid this,

Formula car drivers have their arms strapped in place to defeat the instinct to raise them during a rollover. Sometimes, instinct can be beneficial, but on other occasions it can be disastrous.

Ernest Hemingway claimed there were only three sports for a man to pursue: bull fighting, fishing and auto racing. Two out of three of those sports are dangerous for the participant (of course, the bull is a participant in bullfighting and the fish in fishing, and both face the most danger, but they don't participate voluntarily, so let's limit this discussion to people). I don't know the casualty rate for bullfighters, but I suspect it's lower than competitive car racers.

Racers accept the danger as a reality, but they also refuse to believe the worst will ever happen to them. Why not? Because they are convinced they are better drivers than the other racers, with better eyesight, better reflexes, better strategy and better overall ability. This is understandable. If they didn't think this way, how and why would they ever strap themselves in an open car and drive as fast as possible in the midst of others who are driving the same way?

A Free Pass, a Quiet Exit and a Lesson Learned

For seven years I believed nothing bad could happen to me. And for that length of time, I was right. My skills improved and my confidence grew, especially after I won my first race, an objective it took me a few years to achieve. Then, during a race at Mont-Tremblant in Quebec, it all came down on me, literally.

As I rounded a corner onto a downhill portion of the track, I could see trouble ahead. One car had spun out and its engine had stalled, leaving it blocking the centre of the track. I applied the brakes to slow my car and avoid hitting him, when the wheels of a car beside and slightly behind me touched my rear wheel.

Some law of physics dictates that when the wheel of one car running at speed makes contact with the wheel of another car being slowed by braking, one of the cars will become airborne. In this case, it was mine.

My memory of that instant is perfectly clear. I was upside down and strapped into a car travelling through the air at more than a hundred kilometres per hour. I was looking at the ground as I passed over it, thinking, "This is it. In one second, I will be dead."

The car struck a tree with enough force to bend the forged axle shaft, folding it in half (I salvaged it and kept it on my desk for some time as a souvenir). Thanks to the safety features imposed on Formula Vee cars, I survived without a scratch. Releasing my safety harness, I stepped away from what was left of my car, looked back at the wreckage and told myself I had just received a free pass to keep living.

People who ride horses tell you that, should a horse throw you to the ground, the best thing to do is climb right back into the saddle and keep riding. It may be good advice, but no horse gallops at two miles a minute or drenches you in highly flammable fuel should it roll over.

As I waited for the ambulance to arrive and carry me to the field hospital, I told myself I was not going to climb back behind the wheel of that car—obviously—or any other, for that matter. I was through with racing. I'd had my one victory, and now I had received a free pass. I had my life and my family. I planned to stay around and enjoy both.

I had another reason for abandoning the sport. The accident had stripped me of the veneer of denial, the one that had persuaded me for all those years that it was the other drivers who encountered serious accidents, not me. With that sense of invincibility gone, I would pose a danger to other drivers because my actions would no longer be predictable in dangerous situations.

Travelling through turns at high speeds in open cars, often mere inches from each other, sounds inherently dangerous, and it is. The danger is offset somewhat by each driver's knowledge that all the other drivers have been trained to handle their cars correctly in certain situations. As a result, their actions should be predictable.

When the veneer of denial vanishes, it takes the driver's predictability with it. If I were to return to racing, at some point I would enter a curve at speed, and I wouldn't share the other drivers' confidence that we would all get around the turn safely. Recalling the experience of being both inverted and airborne, I would no longer be predictable—I might lift my foot off the accelerator and touch the brake, surprising the other drivers and creating chaos and disaster all around me.

I couldn't bear to take that risk, so I never raced again.

I took a lot of memories and some satisfaction with me. Taming a powerful vehicle on a crowded racetrack is an amazing experience, worth every penny I invested in the sport, and I may have earned it all back by applying that rule about always looking towards victory and away from potential disaster.

Spinouts and Glaciers

Not only is the The Herjavec Group different from previous companies I've launched, but *I'm* different from the person who launched them. The guy who lived each business day like a non-stop popcorn machine has been replaced by a person better known for his control than his outbursts. I'm still hyper about achieving success, but I have acquired a sense of when it's time to simply listen. I'm learning to listen well.

I'm also learning to recognize that the pace of progress needn't be like a Grand Prix race, with everyone's foot to the floor and a lot of bumps, scrapes and spinouts happening. Sometimes progress advances like a glacier, moving slowly over the ground with little fanfare but lots of stability.

I'm not much for glaciers; I'm more suited to the Grand Prix style. Riding a glacier does not bring out my best qualities as a manager, no matter how much progress is being made. So when the action slows down and frantic turns to steady, I take myself out of the picture and leave things to the staff. No one has yet told me so, but I suspect they're pleased to see me go. They know, of course, that the next hint of a crisis brings me roaring back, with clenched fists and a smile on my face.

46

A Vague Sense of Dissatisfaction

I sympathize with people who are driven to be successful and make the necessary sacrifices, yet find the goal keeps eluding them whenever family obligations come along. They discover they are stuck between two forces pulling with equal strength in opposite directions. Do they abandon their lifelong dream of success, or surrender the joys and satisfaction of close family life? Usually, the choice is to aim for some kind of balance, which means they try to do both. This rarely succeeds, because they're frozen between two desires, neither of which is being satisfied.

Their plight reminds me of a quote attributed to fashion designer Karl Lagerfeld. Despite his lofty position among the top half-dozen leaders in his industry, Lagerfeld claims he is never content with the work he has done or the success he has achieved. "I live in a sort of perpetual dissatisfaction," he says, expressing a point of view I understand perfectly. If success is what you truly desire, you must be prepared to share the same vague sense of dissatisfaction as Lagerfeld.

Stay Out of the Middle

The middle, between your ambition and your obligations, is a very uncomfortable place to be. In my experience, the balanced life can best be achieved by accumulating enough wealth. Family vacations are no difficulty for Diane, my family and me. We enjoy the freedom of time and wherewithal to go where and when we please.

If you manage to succeed in business and achieve a certain level of accumulated assets and annual income, the balanced life you passed up in your earlier years comes within reach. As I mentioned earlier, I continue to sleep only about four hours a night, and my energy level where building my business is concerned remains as high as ever, even though my business achievements no longer need it. Today, if I plan to attend a function where my children are involved and a business situation conflicts with it, I'll assign someone to look after the business matter; unless the situation borders on disaster, I won't cancel the opportunity to be with my children (but I must confess I'd probably stay in touch with staff through my BlackBerry). The rewards I have accumulated from my success enable me to continue this part of my life while satisfying my need to spend time with my wife and children. In that sense, I have achieved balance.

My friend and fellow Dragon Arlene Dickinson was once asked, in an interview, how we Dragons can take so much time away from our "jobs." She replied that we have all learned to work *on* our business, and not *in* our business. A subtle, but important, distinction.

I realize it's easy, having achieved the degree of success I enjoy, to preach that anybody can do it. In truth, not everybody can.

I believe, however, that anybody sufficiently driven to reach a similar goal should be encouraged in every way possible, whether success is likely or not. I cannot imagine anything sadder than someone on their deathbed whispering to themselves, "I didn't even try . . ."

If you honestly wish to explore your business abilities to the maximum, here are three rules to consider. They're my rules, based on my experience, which means they are not necessarily universal. But I believe they can help in your quest to achieve your goal of building a substantial success out of your concepts and ambition.

Rule #1: It is impossible for a born entrepreneur to balance his or her life between the degree of business success desired and the ideal amount of family time needed.

Some people may see this as an anti-family statement, a suggestion that success in business is more important than success at raising a family and enjoying the satisfaction of family life. That's not the way it's intended. I am who I am today in part because of the security and encouragement my family provided me—the unconditional love and support of my mother, the sturdy example of my father, and the standards of hard work and integrity set by my aunts, uncles and grandparents back in Croatia. The centre of my life continues to be my family; no matter how many hours I dedicate to business, they represent the core of my being and identity.

Rule #2: It is easier to put down the roots of success in a new enterprise when the entrepreneur is young and single with few or any outside obligations.

This one's fairly self-explanatory, but not infallible.

Rule #3: If an entrepreneur has not achieved major success by age thirty-five, the likelihood of doing so declines in proportion to his or her age beyond that point.

This is not meant to dissuade older entrepreneurs, but it's a reality that success in business is easier to achieve if you start earlier. By the time you pass age thirty-five, it's difficult to maintain the levels of physical and mental energy needed to keep storming the barriers day after day. At that point it's easier—and, if you have family obligations, probably wiser—to lower your long-term expectations and perhaps hire professional managers to make day-to-day decisions at the firm you had counted on.

And here's a fourth rule: **feel free to ignore rules 2 and 3.** True entrepreneurs are renegades, and renegades ignore rules. Some rules about launching and managing a business should not be disregarded until you have acquired the necessary training and experience to follow your own path, but if you have sufficient drive, ambition and the support of your family, don't let age hold you back. According to some observers, North Americans are rejecting the idea of spending their retirement years on a golf course or a beach and are choosing to fulfill their dreams of being their own boss. The Executive Council for Small Business noted that more than 20 per cent of Canadian business owners are between the ages of forty-six and sixty-two.[3]

An Era of Mature Entrepreneurs?

We may, in fact, be about to enter an era of mature entrepreneurs—folks who may have been ignoring an urge to launch their own companies all their lives and finally make the decision in their fifties and sixties. There could be two reasons for this. One, traditional pension plans are not providing the assured income that many Canadians expected when they entered the work force, and people who wish to retire while they're still active could find themselves needing another income to supplement their limited pensions. And two, we're not only living longer, we're living healthier, more active lives into our seventies and even beyond.

I'm not saying it's going to happen, only that the possibility exists that it *may* happen. On the one hand, I will be pleased if so many people teetering on the brink of becoming their own boss finally seize the opportunity. On the other hand, I fear that late middle age is not the best time for most people to take risks. We have all heard stories of folks who lost everything they owned in a business investment during their thirties and forties and returned to score in a big way. We are unlikely to hear similar stories of people who took the same kinds of risk in their sixties and, when

3 Rick Spence, "Tactics to reach a small business audience," *Financial Post*, November 30, 2009.

things went wrong, rose in a phoenix-like fashion to recover their lost assets.

There are enough exceptions to the rule to encourage those who are truly driven. The best known, perhaps, is Colonel Harland Sanders who, at age sixty-five—when most people choose to retire—first franchised his Kentucky Fried Chicken operation and built it into a food industry powerhouse.

So I'll keep preaching the wisdom of rules 2 and 3 above, and hope I'm proven wrong over and over again.

47

Ensure Support in Your Home Life

The world is littered with shattered marriages that survived the first few years of one driven partner's efforts to achieve his or her goals, but fell apart when the goals were reached. Ironically, the more successful many businesspeople become, the more they need the stability of a supportive spouse and family—another challenge in seeking the benefits of a balanced life.

Things grow more complicated and challenging if your spouse is also your business partner. The challenge of maintaining both a marriage and a business relationship under the stress of a growing business must be enormous.

It works for some people, however. Many years ago, I was in a business partnership with a married couple who operated a successful company together. Both their business and personal relationships appeared to be successful, although I noted that they had decided not to have children, a choice that seems to be popular among other married couples who are also business partners. Another factor in successful business/marriage partnerships: each partner clearly distinguishes his or her prime responsibilities within the company, to reduce the incidence of stepping on each other's toes.

While you may not be able to enjoy the prospect of a balanced life, especially during the early years of a new enterprise, I suspect that the most successful people do not qualify for the stereotype of the self-centred workaholic who never sees his or her family except in passing or by coincidence. Effective businesspeople, in my experience, tend to be more well rounded than that. They may not be able to put their business entirely behind them when they arrive home, but they find time for both, somehow and somewhere.

The most critical aspects of dedicating much of your life to your business while maintaining a healthy and vibrant marriage are the personality of the partners and the nature of the marriage. We have generally rejected the idea of the ideal marriage as a fifty-fifty relationship in favour of a 100-100 partnership. If your spouse relies upon you for 50 per cent of his or her identity and happiness, pulling any part of it away in favour of your business automatically creates strife. On that basis, weak marriages tend to suffer from the stress of running a business, and strong marriages, where each partner is a 100 per cent individual, manage to survive it.

As for me, business never leaves my mind, but neither does my family.

48

Money Will Change You

Money changes people, and entrepreneurs who reach their goals may suddenly find themselves wealthier than they expected (remember that money is a by-product of success, not the primary objective). The change happens, I believe, partially because money and the leisure opportunities it brings foster new levels of introspection on both sides.

When a couple is grappling with financial challenges, either as newlyweds or struggling parents, there's not a heck of lot of time or incentive for them to ask themselves if their lives are being fulfilled. The lack of cash creates its own kind of stress, of course, but although financial problems can create schisms in the relationship, they can also strengthen the bond between the partners, assuming the problems are eventually solved.

People think differently about life when they have a million dollars in their bank account instead of an overdraft, and the difference can be enough to weaken what was once a strong bond. Questions they would have been too busy to ask themselves in the past begin forming in their minds, echoing the old song "Is That All There Is?" If you have all the material things that you once believed would make you happy, and they don't, you may begin looking elsewhere for your happiness. That's my theory, based in part on the large number of friends and colleagues whose marriages appeared stable before they achieved material wealth, but grew shaky after their dreams appeared to be fulfilled.

I'm fortunate in so many ways to have Diane as my spouse. She earned her optometry degree over six strenuous years of study, years that included countless nights of study and work as an intern. She knows what it's like to work eighteen or twenty hours a day in pursuit of a goal; she understands the motivation behind it. Having obtained her degree, she could count on a good income from steady employment, providing an economic safety net if one of my projects went belly-up. This was enormous comfort to both of us, especially during my first years as an entrepreneur. Unless you understand the nature of those driven to succeed—and Diane in her own way shares a drive similar to my own and continues to work with similar levels of effort—it can be difficult to share your life with them.

49

Change What You Can, Tolerate What You Must

I admit it: I'm an impatient guy. When things need to be done now, I want them done yesterday. I make no apologies about it. Impatience, directed where it's truly needed, is at least partially responsible for the success I've achieved.

Over the years, I have learned to aim my impatience at areas and actions that I can influence. Those who know me, and know about my lack of patience in many areas, are often surprised at my ability to do this.

While driving with three members of my company to an important sales call, we encountered one of the enormous traffic jams Toronto is becoming famous for. There we were, frozen in place like some prehistoric creatures in a glacier, and my three colleagues were having mini heart attacks about being late for the meeting, missing the chance to close the sale, and so on. Meanwhile, I remained calm.

Finally, one of the others looked at me in amazement and said, "I can't believe you're okay with this traffic mess."

I explained to him that I was definitely not okay with the traffic, but that I had learned over the years not to become frustrated with things I can't control—like traffic, government and bank policies. Forget about changing them. Instead, learn what the rules are and use them to your benefit.

Governments are difficult to deal with in most cases—that's a given. If you're prepared to deal with the red tape, they can be a terrific help in developing export markets. At The Herjavec Group, we don't spend a lot of time railing against government rules. We prefer to spend the time building our business. Banks have their bureaucracy as well, but once you appreciate their position in detail it's easier to accept their demands on you and your firm. Understanding, in this case, is much easier and more productive than revising, or attempting to.

Blasting your car's horn in a traffic jam doesn't work. I don't see any benefit in taking similar actions with governments and banks. Like rush-hour traffic, they are essentially immovable. Besides, more can be gained by addressing small, incremental improvements in a corporation. That's where day-to-day efforts should be directed.

If you were to ask a world-class sprinter in his or her prime years to name their objective, they might respond, "To win a gold medal at the Olympics." Ask them what their goal is this week, and their answer will likely identify some technical action that needs correcting or improving, such as positioning their driving leg differently for the start or angling their body out of the blocks. They want that gold medal hanging around their neck while their eyes fill with tears at the sound of their national anthem. But they won't reach that great, glorious moment without spending the hours needed to hone a thousand little details.

My goal is to build a great company that is large enough, innovative enough and stable enough to stand the test of time. If I succeed, I'll do it the same way the sprinter plans to do it: by making a small improvement today, followed by another tomorrow, and on and on. Like sprinting and swimming and a dozen other athletic challenges, success will always be achieved by making minuscule improvements on a grand scale.

50

There Is No Finish Line

Businesspeople prepare themselves for their careers in various ways. Some, by being born within a business-based family, gain insights by osmosis, from watching and helping their parents run the family enterprise. Others build their abilities through education, with university courses and post-graduate work towards an MBA or other accreditation. A few of us find our way through practical experience, delighting in our successes and learning from our failures.

After all these takes and observations I've covered, it may be wise to list the steps I feel are most critical. These are not necessarily the same ones you encounter in other books, and a few have been influenced by my experience on *Dragons' Den*. Some have already been mentioned, but they bear mentioning again.

- **Love what you do.** If you honestly love your profession or career, you'll never be "going to work." You'll always be going to play.

- **Money is great, but it's never the sole reward.** Every outstanding business success, from Nike shoes to Four Seasons Hotels, was the product of one driven individual's dream, vision and determination.
- **Fill a defined need or requirement.** Identify a product or service that serves a known market in a unique manner. It needn't be entirely new, but it has to be new to the market it serves.
- **Base your business decisions on facts, not opinions.** Enthusiasm is a wonderful quality, but driving blind is unwise, whether it's behind the wheel or behind a desk. Too many people are blinded by their zeal to get started. Investigate the competitive, technical, financial and legal aspects of the business you're considering before investing a penny in launching it.
- **Trust customers to know what they need and want.** Everything you do in business must be in response to your customers. No matter how wonderful you feel your product or service may be, if it doesn't strike a strong enough chord with enough customers in your market, you will fail. Satisfy your customers first.
- **Don't overestimate the number of your customers or underestimate the time they will take to award you their business.** It is far easier for a prospect to say you have her business than it is for her to actually make the decision. Keep your expectations within reason.
- **Your life is not that hard—you can always do more.** My parents arrived from Croatia in their mid-thirties with me, twenty dollars in cash and no ability to speak English. They succeeded, which encouraged me to succeed. On a more

contemporary note, I recently met a Canadian soldier who lost both legs on the battlefield in Afghanistan. His first words after waking up in the hospital were, "When can I go back?" To prove he was capable of serving, he ran a marathon on prosthetic legs two years after being wounded. You are not, I suspect, as badly off as you may think.

- **Smile.** It reassures your friends and confuses your enemies. It's also infectious.
- **Learn from others.** Acquire knowledge that has been gained before you and leave wisdom for those who come after you.
- **Never give up.** Winston Churchill kept repeating that phrase to himself, and others, from 1939 to 1945. It worked then. It works now.

Five Questions for Up-and-Running Companies

Any company that lacks strong, decisive leadership is basically coasting. And things coast when they are either going downhill or running out of fuel. To prevent your company from coasting, consider asking yourself five questions on a regular basis—monthly, quarterly or annually. Here are the questions. Only you can supply the answers.

1. **Where are we now?** What are our sales and profits?
2. **Where are we headed?** Are our sales growing or shrinking? What shape is the market in?
3. **What are our options?** Do we add or eliminate products or services? Look for new facilities or financing? Expand or contract? Diversify or refocus?

4. **What guidelines do we follow?** Can we set reachable goals? Is our time frame adequate? Can our staff handle the challenge?

5. **How do we implement the guidelines?** Will we need new research or training? Will staff and customers accept the change?

What Will You Leave Behind?

Successful businesspeople who accumulate substantial assets and a high profile in the community are expected to "give back" something to society. The idea is to recognize that their achievements provide them with the opportunity to assist others who, for whatever reason, may benefit from the cash contributions that wealthy people can provide.

I'm all in favour of the idea. But I believe that everyone in similar circumstances to my own should determine for themselves how they "give back," and act according to their own nature. Many, for example, enjoy building hospital wings or community facilities bearing their name. That's fine, but public display is not my style. Whatever assistance I offer will be, for the most part, private and low-key. I confess that I enjoy some of the recognition that my work and my appearances on *Dragons' Den* bring, but I'm not interested in achieving fame for whatever good deeds I perform.

I also believe that many of the causes Diane and I support can benefit as much or more from actions and attitudes than from writing cheques. In addition to making cash contributions, we have used our home on several occasions, for example, as the site of fundraising events in support of cancer research and other causes, and I know we will continue to do so.

None of us can save the world on our own, of course. We can save only the corners we reside in, or the ones we choose. I could fill this book with good causes and still not cover every need that exists. Like it or not, we are forced to choose the causes on which we'll focus our resources.

So, what is our legacy?

In my case, it will be our children. I hope Diane and I have influenced our children to act with wisdom, integrity and all the corny, old-fashioned standards that have been valued since our grandparents' day and beyond. Our resources will provide them with opportunities to reach whatever heights their abilities and ambitions might take them. That combination of strong principles and great achievements, I trust, will enable them to positively influence all the corners of the world they choose to explore, multiplying the impact accordingly.

That's what I choose to leave behind—not my name carved on a pile of bricks and mortar, but my values, in business and in personal relationships, embedded in their actions.

Slow Down? I'm Still Sprinting

Whatever my legacy, it will have value and, like all things of value in life, it has come with a price. The price has been worth it to me. I have to ensure that it is also worth it to those around me, because I cannot slow down and let others catch up. If you cannot run with me, you will run behind me, and the longer the run, the farther you'll fall behind.

This makes it a challenge for others—including, at times, my colleagues and family. They would like the pace to ease for a while, and I understand that. I cannot change my driven style. It hasn't changed in twenty-five years, and I cannot imagine it changing in the next twenty-five. It probably will, but it's beyond my ability to conceive of it.

I am like the sprinter who spends each day searching for new ways of exploding out of the blocks at the precise moment the starter's gun fires, of leaping ahead of everyone else, of focusing all his attention and energy on hitting the finish line, breaking the ribbon and stopping the clock in front of everybody else competing against him.

Here is the difference between that sprinter and me:

I have no finish line.